Imagine you have a friend in New Delhi. Someone who has enthusiastically explored the city to discover its best experiences, its sights, dining and shopping, who leads you through colonial tree-lined boulevards, tangled medieval alleys and mystifying spice markets, sharing knowledge and making recommendations along the way.

Your guide, Kirsten Ellis, has been based in New Delhi for nearly four years as a writer on Indian life and culture.

Insight Pocket Guide: New Delhi is for the active traveler who wants the optimum pleasure from a visit to New Delhi. Ellis begins with an overview of New Delhi's history and describes the majestic relics of 3,000 year-old empires. She explains its intrigue-ridden and unwieldy democracy, and shows life that's every bit as Indian and as astonishing, exhausting and exhilarating as the most demanding traveler could ask.

The author then offers three full-day itineraries to familiarize you with New Delhi. The first begins with a tour of the magnificent Raj-era architecture, Arc de Triomphe-like India Gate and a visit to an extraordinary 18-century astronomical observatory, followed by a stroll around Connaught Place's colonial hub to browse in treasure-laden shops, ending with an Indian dinner at a superb restaurant.

These itineraries, which incorporate major places of interest, like the Taj Mahal in Agra, are followed by 14 morning, afternoon and evening excursions for you to combine as you please. Whether you plunge into the city's tumultuous street-life, go on a serious shopping foray or enjoy a peaceful walk through picturesque ruins in the countryside, you'll find the insights and perceptions offered by Ellis informative and useful. She also suggests where to break for lunch, and which off-beat sights or events will make your visit more memorable. Her advice on how to deal, light-heartedly, with "Delhi-belly", intelligently, with "genuine" antiques and more seriously, how not to offend Delhites, among many others, stem from the hindsight of her experiences, and ensure that you adopt some necessary street savvy and avoid common pitfalls.

The purpose of this book is to help you discover and enjoy this idiosyncratic city for yourself. The itineraries should act as a catalyst, not as a straight jacket. You are encouraged to depart from them from time to time as whim takes you. Happy exploring!

Welcome! Namaste!

Insight Pocket Guide:
NewDelhi
First Edition

© **1991 APA Publications (HK) Ltd**

All Rights Reserved

Printed in Singapore by

Höfer Press (Pte) Ltd

INSIGHT *POCKET* GUIDES

Recommendations for a Short Stay

NEW DELHI

Written by	**Kirsten Ellis**
Directed by	**Hans Höfer**
Design Concept by	**V. Barl**
Art Direction by	**Karen Hoisington**
Photography by	**Pankaj Shah**
Editorial Director	**Michael Stachels**

A P A
INSIGHT
GUIDES

Contents

Welcome..3
Introduction..**10**
History and Culture **12**
Delhi: cities lost and found **12**
Landmarks **16**
A few milestones **17**

Day Itineraries
Day 1: Getting acquainted **21**
Day 2: Mosques and moneylenders **26**
Day 3: Time-worn tombs **34**
Pick and Choose
A.M. Itineraries
1. Ruins, rattlesnakes and rose petals **40**
2. Monkey and markets **46**
3. Spices, sweetmeats and shrines **49**
4. Culture backgrounder **54**
5. Fortress foray **57**
6. Memories of the Raj................................**59**
7. Buygones: antiques and curio hunting **64**
8. Sultanpur Bird Sanctuary **67**

P.M. Itineraries

    9. Away from the crowds **68**

    10. Sunday tour **70**

    11. Ruins and a temple **73**

    12. On the Gandhi and Nehru trail **73**

    13. Suraj Kund **77**

Nightlife **78**

Day Trips

    Agra and Fatehpur Sikri **80**

Dining Experiences

    Breakfast **84**

    Lunch **85**

    Afternoon tea **85**

    Evening cocktails **86**

    A taste of India **86**

    Where To Dine Like A Maharajah (Mughlai

    and North Indian food) **87**

    Open-air dining **88**

    South Indian Vegetarian **89**

    Others **89**

Shopping

    The Government Emporia **93**

    What to buy where **94**

Calendar of Special Events **100**

What To Know

Travel Essentials **104**
Getting Acquainted **107**
Getting Around **110**
Where To Stay **112**
Hours Of Business and Public Holidays **114**
Health and Emergency **114**
Communications and News **115**
Special Information **117**
Useful Addresses **118**
Further Reading **122**

Maps

India **2**
Day 1 .... **20**
Day 2 .... **27**
Day 3 .... **35**
A.M. Itinerary **40**
A.M. Itinerary **45**
A.M. Itinerary **49**
Delhi **127**

When I was told in 1986 that my foreign correspondent boy-friend was being posted to Delhi, I packed my bags in a mood of rash excitement, telling myself that whatever happened was bound to be an adventure. Arriving for the first time in India was like being transported into a heightened zone of sensory bombardment. First, one's nostrils had to adjust to the distinctive wafts of incense, rotting refuse and sunbaked dung. Then, driving in from the airport, there was the fascinated horror of being plunged into darkness and near-anarchic traffic by a bearded, be-turbanned taxi driver, his dashboard adorned with plastic flowers and dangling flywhisks, who swerved us safely through an over-heated mystifying mad-house of bazaars and bicycles, crowds and cattle, dust and decay.

Waking up the next morning in a slightly frayed colonial hotel, I remember the novelty of being served an omelette and cardamom-sweet tea by a cummerbund-clad waiter with a walrus moustache, a cap of raggedy plumes and a seemingly inexhaustible supply of broad head-waggling smiles. Turning to the newspapers was to be alter-nately bemused by the dense Edwardian prose and startled by banner headlines proclaiming both the violent and bizarre, as well as the merely commonplace. Dacoits Storm Train Killing 50. Girl (8) Cuts Out Own Tongue for Lord Shiva. Government Minister Sacks Peons. Whenever I looked up, a gecko lizard cocked its head from the bedroom wall. I was beginning to feel quite at home.

As the days turned into weeks, then months, the fascination of living amid Delhi's colorful, sometimes perplexing chaos never left me, even when temperatures soared, the days baked and fans wheezed to a halt in the frequent power cuts. The search to unravel the city's secrets became an addiction and a form of amusement.

It took me, countless times; to the old walled city and its centuries-old maze of teeming junk bazaars. I was absorbed by the fragments of life glimpsed through paint-splintered doors. Kohl-eyed Muslim boys in green alcoves memorizing their prayers in Urdu. Merchants who looked like oriental pashas on their ottoman cushions while women in bright saris fingered their gold jewelry and brocade silks.

Ash-smeared holy men squatting next to banyan trees smoking their *chillum* pipes. Traders bent over stacks of ledgers, shouting in archaic telephones over the din. It was here, amid the dust-laden light and endless movement, that the city revealed its true personality of free-wheeling enterprise and joyful confusion.

When the crowds, noise and dirt became too oppressive, I retreated to the agreeable sanctity of British-built New Delhi, with its pompous colonial architecture, broad tamarind tree-lined boulevards and polished mausoleum-style five-star hotels. New Delhi exhibits an extreme contrast between a sort of living medievalism and 1930s modernity. That it still manifests a perceptible hangover from the Raj era, was always for me, its most idiosyncratic and endearing charm. It was not at all surprising to learn that the P.G. Wodehouse enjoys a cult following among Delhi's rich and powerful, many of whom live in old bungalows with a household of family retainers.

You will find that Delhi is really two distinct cities merged into one. And that seven successive cities have existed here. Ruins are as commonplace as traffic lights, casting a shadow of pervasive antiquity wherever you look. The city's contemporary skyline betrays its own contradictions, with its centuries-old monuments, lapis-domed mosques and magnificent forts surrounded by embassies and stark concrete tenements.

You need time to take it all in, and a measure of stamina too. But you'll find, like me, that once you start digging beneath a city's surface, curiosity is always the best guide and its own reward.

Kirsten Ellis.

Delhi: cities lost and found

Delhi is layered in antiquity. At almost every step, some majestic, centuries-old relic of a fallen empire looms within sight. Abandoned fortresses are fringed by concrete tenements, tombs of the once-powerful have become grazing places for goats and the might of fabled dynasties are remembered only as street names.

As India's capital and its third largest city, Delhi is literally a living museum paved with almost three thousand years of history. No less than seven successive cities have risen and decayed here, each superimposed on the last. Archaeologists poking through the rubble are always finding new ones, and the latest tally seems to be fourteen, adding to the surfeit of dates, dynasties and kings

The story of Delhi begins with grey pottery shards unearthed near the 16th-century site of Purana Qila, which indicate that a settlement existed on the banks of the Yamuna river around 1000 B.C. Later stone inscriptions confirm the existence of a city by 300 B.C., and it's said that this was the legendary city of Indraprastha, built by the Pandavas, mythical heroes in the famous Hindu epic detailing the Hindu philosophy of life, the *Mahabharata*.

Invading Hindu Rajput dynasties were responsible for the first "Dilli's", whose rocky islands of ruins are scattered across the far reaches of south Delhi. The earliest known structure is that of Suraj Kund, 10 miles (16 km) away, a vast 10th-century Romanesque-style amphitheater with broad steps leading down to a pool. Built by the Tomar Rajputs, it's thought to have been dedicated to Surya, the sun god. The Tomars also built Delhi's first city, Lal Kot, around where the Qutb Minar stands today, and brought the Iron Pillar to Delhi.

Feudal battles ensured that Lal Kot soon fell to another Hindu Rajput clan, the Chauhans, in the 12th century, led by the hero-king Rai Pithora, who built massive ramparts around the settlement and re-named it Qila Rai Pithora. He was defeated and be-headed in 1191 by Muhammad Ghori of Afghanistan, who became the first Muslim

to establish an empire in India. Ghori installed his former slave, Qutb-ud-din-Aibak, to the seat of power and Aibak established the so-called Slave dynasty in 1206.

Aibak tore his predecessor's city to rubble, then set to work building the Quwwat-ul-Islam, one of India's first mosques, built from the remains of 27 Hindu temples with the looted Iron Pillar given pride of place in its courtyard – and his famous tower of victory, the Qutb Minar.

The Slave dynasty ended in 1296, when Sultan Ala-ud-din of the Afghan Khiljis established a new one, and built Delhi's second city of Siri, which lay a few miles north-west of Lal Kot and is now completely lost.

By 1321, the Afghan Khijis were ousted by the formidable Muslim Tughlaqs, a bulldog-breed of warriors who constructed no fewer

13th-century gateway – Alai Darwaza

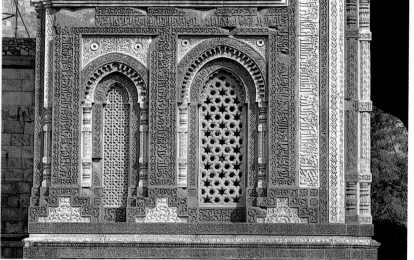

Early morning jog in Lodhi Gardens

than three cities during the 14th century. The first, Tughlaqabad, built by Ghiyas-ud-Din, is now a ruined ghost city, dotted with tombs and enclosed by sloping battlements.

Within five years of his reign, Ghiyas-ud-Tughlaq was succeeded by his son, Muhammed-bin-Tughlaq, who built Jahanpanah, and then acting on imperial whim, decided to transfer his capital to Daulatabad in the Deccan, 685 miles (1100 km) away. Like the mad "grand old Duke of York" he force-marched his subjects all they way there, and then after an interval, marched them all back to Delhi again.

Delhi's fifth city of Firozabad was the final and most impressive achievement of the Tughlaq rulers, founded in 1451, by Muhammed's cousin, Feroz Shah. His 37-year long reign was largely peaceful, and he was able to indulge in his hobby for building and repairing the existing buildings of the Qutb complex. Although most of the large and prosperous city was demolished by Shah Jahan in the 17th century, you can still see the citadel of Feroz Shah Kotla, with its ruined palace, mosque and one of the two third-century Ashokan pillars transported to Delhi by Feroz Shah.

When the Tughlaq line weakened after Feroz Shah's death, Delhi was ransacked by Timur the Lane, emir of Samarkand, whose army spent two weeks looting and murdering, then returned home. Power passed to the Sayyids, descendents of the Prophet, who barely made a dent in Delhi's history and to three generations of Pathan Lodhi kings who built Delhi's sixth city. All that remains of this city is the necropolis of beautiful tombs, mosques and monuments now enclosed by the Lodhi Gardens.

The first of the Great Mughals to arrive in Delhi was Babur, an Afghan warlord who defeated the last of the Afghan Lodhis, Sultan Ibrahim, at the historic battle of Panipat in 1526.

That marked the start of the Mughal empire, the most dazzling, affluent and decadent period of India's history, which reached its zenith while Queen Elizabeth I ruled England. Throughout India, but especially in Delhi and Agra, the Mughals left a legacy of magnificent palaces, fortress cities, tombs and landscaped gardens, including India's most famous building, the Taj Mahal.

Babur's son, Humayan, started building Delhi's sixth city, choosing the site of ancient Indraprastha on the western bank of the Yamuna. He laid the foundation stone in 1533 and named his new city Din Panah (Haven of Faith), but was ousted by an energetic Afghan chieftain, Sher Shah Suri, who had established himself in Bengal and Bihar. Humayan fled ignominiously to Persia, using the Koh-i-noor to bribe his way out to safety. The usurper built many roads as well as much of the sixth city of Delhi, known as Purana

Qila, before Humayan reclaimed the throne in 1555. You can see Humayan's impressive tomb, a precursor to the Taj Mahal, near Nizamuddin village.

Humayan's son, Akbar, became the greatest Mughal ruler, choosing to make his capital in Agra where he built a massive, crenellated fort. A brand-new city at Fatehpur Sikri, 23 miles (37 km) west of Agra, served as his home for just 15 years.

Not until 1638 did Delhi become the capital of the Mughal empire. After Shah Jahan had enlarged Agra Fort and built the magnificent Taj Mahal, he decided to embark on Delhi's seventh city, which he called Shahjahanabad. He personally supervised the construction of his city, for which masons and craftsmen were brought from all over the empire.

You can see his massive Red Fort, with its once sumptuous palace quarters, which surveys the giant Jama Masjid mosque and the broad processional avenue, Chandni Chowk, or "Moonlit Crossing," that was laid out by Shah Jahan's daughter, Jahanara Begum. A wide canal once ran down the center, flanked by merchants' *havelis*, or houses, and pretty gardens – a far cry from today's noisy, chaotic bustle of rickshaws and tangled stalls.

A century later, Delhi was ravaged by the ruthless Persian king Nadir Shah in 1739, and the Mughal empire fell into decay.

In 1837, the British placed the last Mughal, the blind old poet Bahudur Shah, under their yoke, stripping him of all effective power but leaving him his title and throne. The early colonials settled in Civil Lines, north of old Delhi near Delhi University, an area still greatly redolent of the early Raj, with its decaying old bungalows and musty graveyards.

To the south of the old city, the British colonial masters laid out New Delhi during the early 20th century as their new purpose-built capital, shifting the seat of power from Calcutta. Begun in 1911, the

Secretariat, masterpiece by Lutyens

mammoth project was finally completed in 1931 at a cost of 15 million pounds. This "eighth city" of Delhi was built to accommodate 70,000 people and was designed by Sir Edwin Lutyens and his assistant Herbert Baker. More than 30,000 unskilled laborers were hired and a staggering 700 million bricks used.

After Independence, New Delhi has continued expanding at a rapid rate. Villages that were once considered outposts on the periphery of Delhi have gradually been swallowed by the concrete jungle, yet still exist like little pockets of living history, such as Nizamuddin. At heart, Delhi is a city of bureaucracy and politics, playing host to the nation's powerful elite – *khadi*-wearing politicians, sleek industrialists and chaffeur-driven diplomats. Yet it defies homogenization, and retains a unique Indian-ness of spirit everywhere.

Landmarks

Visitors to Delhi immediately remark on the immense contrast between the city's ancient and modern character, for this is really two distinct cities rolled into one.

New Delhi's grid-like boulevards are relatively easy to find your way around – roads are well-signed, and all the street names uniformly belong to the post-Independence era – but it is very spread out, so it can feel as if you spend most of your time getting from one place to another. The imperial Rashtrapati Bhavan complex lies at the center of New Delhi, linked to India Gate by the sweeping avenue of Rajpath. From this radiate concentric rings of tree-lined streets, ministries, bungalows and landscaped gardens. Many of the city's hotels lie within this residential area of New Delhi. Further north lies the central hub of Connaught Place – with its concentric rows of colonaded shops – which forms the city's commercial heart, and where most banks, airline offices and shops are found. A little further north is the Paharganj area, with its reputation as a back-packers haunt, close to the New Delhi Railway Station.

The historic medieval city of Old Delhi has the Red Fort and the Jama Masjid as its major landmarks, very near to the Old Delhi Railway Station.

The Red Fort by night

History

BC 1200: Pottery shards discovered in 1955 on the site of Purana Qila give substance to the myth that Delhi may have been the original site of the legendary city of Indraprastha, "Abode of India", founded by the Pandava brothers as recounted in the epic *Mahabharata*.

The Rajput Period (900-1200)

Circa 900: Surajpal of the Tomar Hindu Rajput clan constructs Suraj Kund, a sun-worshipping amphitheater-pool south of Delhi. Anangpal, another Tomar chieftain, builds Lal Kot, said to be Delhi's first city.

1192-3: The Afghan invader, Muhammed of Ghor, triumphs over the Chauhans and retires to his native land, leaving his slave Qutb-ud-Din Aibak behind to become Delhi's first Muslim ruler. Qutb-ud-Din starts building the Quwwat-i-Islam mosque from the remains of 27 demolished Hindu and Jain temples from Lal Kot.

1199: Qutb-ud-Din lays the foundations of the Qutb Minar as his tower of victory, or as a minaret to call the faithful to prayer; completed later by his son-in-law and successor, Iltutmish (1211-1236).

The Delhi Sultanate (1206-1526)

1206-1303: Qutb-ud-Din enthrones himself at Lahore as the first sultan of Delhi and starts the line known as the Slave Kings.

This dynasty ends in 1296 when Feroz Shah, a Turk of the Afghan Khalji tribe in the Delhi court, stages a *coup*. He assumes the Sultanate mantle and the new Khalji dynasty under the name Ala-ud-Din, captures the Rajput fortress of Chittor, and founds Delhi's second city, a few miles east of Lal Kot. He also excavates the huge reservoir at Hauz Khas.

1321-1351: Ghiyas-ud-Din Tughlaq, a Turk noble, stages an assault and is proclaimed sultan. He founds the Tughlaq dynasty, the third in the Delhi Sultanate and starts building Tughlaqabad, the third city of Delhi. In 1325, his son, Muhammed-bin Tughlaq, assumes power and builds Jahanpanah, the fourth city, between Lal Kot and Siri. In 1351, Feroz Shah Tughlaq, Muhammed's nephew, builds Firozabad, the fifth city on the western banks of the Yamuna River.

1414: The last of the Tughlaqs dies, and power passes to Sayyids, descendents of the Prophet, the fourth of the Delhi Sultanates.

1451: An Afghan noble, Buhlbal Lodi, captures the throne and founds the Lodi dynasty, the last of the Delhi Sultanates. Sikander, the dynasty's second ruler, shifts his capital near Agra, and builds a new city which he names after himself.

The Mughal Dynasty (1526-1857)

1526: Babur, a feudal overlord from Samarkand, sweeps across north India from Afghanistan. At the Battle of Panipat, his army kills Ibrahim Lodi and 20,000 soldiers, laying the road open for Delhi and Agra where the young warlord proudly proclaims himself the first Mughal emperor.

1540: 23-year old Humayan succeeds his father, and starts building Purana Qila, Delhi's sixth city, but is soon ousted from his throne by an Afghan commoner, Sher Shah Suri, who captures Delhi after slaughtering 8,000 Mughal soldiers. Sher Shah completes much of Purana Qila before Humayan returns from exile and successfully wrests back the throne in 1555.

1556: Akbar is enthroned at the age of 14, after Humayan falls to his death from his library stairs at Purana Qila. Through a series of military campaigns he pushes the borders of the Mughal empire three-quarters of the way across the sub-continent. Until his death in 1605 he is known as "Akbar the Great."

1565: Akbar starts building the Red Fort in his capital city of Agra.

1569: Akbar begins work on Fatehpur Sikri, 23 miles (37 km) west of Agra.

1574: Fatehpur Sikri, Akbar's "dream city", is completed and the capital shifts there from Agra.

1584: The Mughlal court returns to Agra, apparently because a shortage of water in Fatehpur Sikri. Akbar starts building his tomb at Sikandra where he is later buried. He is succeeded by Jahangir, who rules from 1605-1627 and Shah Jahan, ruler from 1627-1658.

1600: Queen Elizabeth I grants a trading charter to the British East India Company, and eight years later the corporation of wealthy English merchants sets up its first port settlement at Surat in Gujarat.

1632-1654: Shah Jahan builds the Taj Mahal.

1638: Shah Jahan transfers the capital from Agra to Delhi and lays the foundations for Shahjahanabad, the seventh city. He also begins work in 1639 on Lal Qila, the Red Fort, completing his city in 1648.

1659: Aurangzeb is crowned in Delhi after gaining victory over his brothers. Shah Jahan is imprisoned in the Red Fort at Agra, beside the Yamuna river and overlooking the Taj Mahal, until his death in 1666.

1707: Aurangzeb dies. The Mughal empire slowly decays.

1739: Nadir Shah, a Persian king, invades Delhi and slaughters more than 30,000 people in Shahjahanabad before returning to Persia with the symbol of Mughal glory, the Peacock Throne.

1857: The Indian Mutiny breaks out in Meerut, where sepoys are incited by a rumor that new bullets being issued are greased with animal fat from pigs, which are unclean to Muslims, and cows, which are scared to Hindus. The anti-British campaign rapidly spreads across India, and much blood is spilt on both sides. By the year's end, the British quell the rebellion and exact revenge in Delhi. Bahaudur Shah, the last Mughal emperor, is exiled to Burma.

The British Raj (1858-1947)

1858: The British Crown imposes direct rule over India, abolishing the East India Company, where, until 1947, a Viceroy becomes the sovereign's representative and chief executive.

1877: Queen Victoria is proclaimed Sovereign Empress of India.

1911: On 12 December, George V, King and Emperor, announces at Delhi's Durbar that the capital of British India will be transferred from Calcutta to Delhi.

1915: Mohandas Gandhi, who subsequently becomes known as Mahatma, or "great soul", returns from South Africa and campaigns for passive resistance, *satyagraha*, to British rule.

1919: General Dyer orders his

Gurkha troops to open fire on a peaceful but illegal Indian anti-British protest meeting in Amritsar, killing 379 people and wounding 1,200 in the sealed courtyard of Jalianwala Bagh. This proves catalytic to the Indian independence movement, and a year later, Indian nationalists launch their Non-Cooperation Movement against British rule.

1930: Mahatma Gandhi's "Quit India" drive gains momentum with his famous Dandi Salt March from Ahmedabad to protest taxes on Indian-produced salt.

1931: New Delhi is formerly inaugurated as the capital of India.

Independence
(1948- Present)

1947: India gains its independence from Britain at midnight, 15 August. Jawaharlal Nehru becomes India's first Prime Minister.

In the aftermath of the power transfer, the subcontinent is sliced into two new nations, creating Pakistan and India. In the months-long upheavals triggered by partition, more than ten million people migrated in each direction across the divided Punjab – the largest human exodus in history. Communal violence between Hindus, Sikhs and Muslims claims between 200,000 to one million lives.

1948: Mahatma Gandhi goes on a prolonged hunger strike advocating reconciliation and an end to communal violence.

He is assassinated on 30 January by a Hindu fanatic. The horrific incident shames the nation and places it under shock. It loses the will for blood-letting and allows Nehru to turn his attention to the task of building a new India.

1950: The Constitution of India comes into force on 26 January.

1964: Nehru dies, and one year later, his successor, Lal Bahadur Shastri, successfully repulses Pakistan's twin attacks on India – one in the Rann of Kutch, the other in Kashmir.

1966: Indira Gandhi, Nehru's daughter (no relation to Mahatma) becomes the first woman prime minister of India.

1971: Agitation in East Pakistan erupts into war, and after 12 days of fighting, Pakistan agrees to the creation of the new independent Bangladesh nation.

1975-1977: Indira Gandhi imposes an 18-month State of Emergency, involving suspension of civil liberties and imprisonment of hundreds of her political opponents. In 1977 she is defeated in national elections, and Moraji Desai of the Opposition's Janata Party becomes Prime Minister in March.

1980: Indira Gandhi returns as Prime Minister in January.

1984: Some 1,000 people die when the Indian army storms the Golden Temple in Amritsar, the holiest Sikh shrine. The carnage and desecration of the shrine enrage Sikhs and results in the 31 October retaliatory assassination of Indira Gandhi by two of her Sikh bodyguards. That unleashes a backlash by Hindus, leaving more than 2,700 Sikhs dead in riots in Delhi in the first three days of November.

Indira's son, Rajiv Gandhi, calls elections in December and is swept into power with a landslide victory.

1989: In November elections, Rajiv Gandhi loses his mandate to the Opposition, and Vishwanath Pratap Singh, the leader of the National Front, becomes Prime Minister of India.

Day itinerary

Most first-time visitors to India find they take a couple of days to adjust to its unfamiliar climate, pace and culture. Even exploring your immediate surroundings can trigger sensory overkill for some. By the end of your first three days in Delhi, you'll have sampled the city's endearingly idiosyncratic atmosphere and charm, and seen many of its key sights. Always stray if something interesting beckons – the planned tours are not intended as a straitjacket, but as a catalyst for your enjoyment of the city.

Although Delhiites tend to wake with the sun, the city's offices, shops and museums don't start bustling until at least 10 a.m. This is usually a good time to set out on a day of sightseeing. If the suggested itineraries seem to cram too much in one day, concentrate instead on what interests you. Like the rest of India, Delhi is best

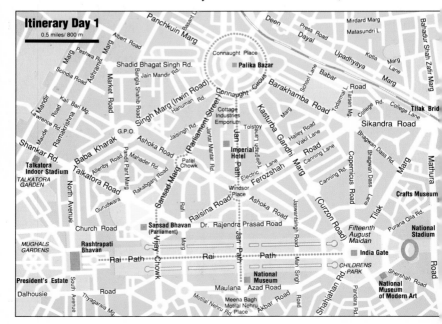

Indian and British troops remembered

appreciated on a loose schedule and at your own pace. For the first few days, I've suggested that you eat out mainly at hotel restaurants – where, it should be noted, you'll be sampling some of the city's best dining experiences. Generally, hotels maintain a good standard of hygiene, and it's wise to safeguard yourself against "Delhi Belly", especially during your first few days after arrival.

Getting acquainted

Taxi to India Gate; Rashtrapati Bhavan; Jantar Mantar; crafts-browsing in Connaught Place; lunch at Hotel Imperial. Take a map of the city.

Your first foray should be tackled at a leisurely pace, giving you time to work off any lingering jet-lag. Today of all days, take it gently. The tour will whisk you around the concentric rings of New

Delhi's spacious tree-lined boulevards, offering glimpses of remarkable relics of colonial architecture, landscaped gardens and the inner city's chaotic streetlife. By the end of the day, you'll be able to get your bearings around the central hub of Connaught Place, where all the banks, shops, tourist and airline offices and many tourist-orientated restaurants and hotels are found.

Have a relaxed start with a leisurely breakfast at your hotel. Fresh *musumbi* (sweet lime) juice, papaya, chilled yoghurt, and delicious real South-Indian coffee (not unpalatable instant coffee) are the best choices. Set off at about 10 a.m. and hire a taxi for the morning, which should come to about Rs150.

Start with **India Gate**. The Arc de Triomphe-like 138-feet (42-meter) high memorial arch was built by the British in 1931 to honor the 60,000 Indians who died in World War I and the 13,516 British and Indian troops who died fighting along the Northwest Frontier in the ill-fated 1919 Third Afghan War. Under the arch, an eternal flame burns alongside the inverted bayonet and helmet of the Unknown Soldier – recent additions made by Indira Gandhi after the Third Indo-Pakistan War in 1971. Close by is the empty canopy which once housed a statue of King George V, which has been removed to Coronation Memorial, north of Old Delhi.

Rajpath, or Kingsway, is the stately avenue that runs for 2 miles (3.2 km) down to Rashtrapati Bhavan, flanked by the Maidan, a sprawling green flanked by two canals. On hot summer days, bullocks recover from their lawn-mowing exertions and dhoti-clad workmen play cards beneath leafy trees.

At night, the **Maidan** is a magnet for lolling families, courting couples and hawkers of ice-cream, candy-floss and sweet-scented jasmine garlands. The **Delhi Boat Club** is tucked away near the right canal, popular for floating toy vessels, and – after the monsoon swell – rowing dinghies in the shallow canal. Demonstrations take place here at least once a week, with a battery of placards, burning effigies and slogan-shouting, often swelling to completely clog the inner-city traffic. They are staged with prior police permission by just about every disgruntled faction imaginable – from Afghan or Tibetan refugees to striking income tax collectors.

At the end of Rajpath is Vijay Chowk's forum-style expanse at the bottom of the sloping **Raisana Hill**, where the gloriously imperial "Beating The Retreat" ceremony with camel-mounted soldiers is held at dusk every January. (See Calendar of Special Events). As your taxi climbs up the slope, Chief Architect Sir Edwin Lutyen's **Rashtrapati Bhavan**, built as the Viceregal Palace, looms straight ahead, while his assistant Herbert Baker's twin **Secretariats**, decorated with pagoda-style domes, stand to your left and right.

Wedding at Hotel Arun Anand

The entire complex – which required some 30,000 laborers, both men and women – was inaugurated in 1931, and has been called the single greatest artifact of the British Empire. However, a furious Lutyens claimed he had met his "Bakerloo" when his assistant miscalculated the steep gradient upon which this sprawling architectural power symbol stands. Official parsimony compounded the error, the result of which obscured the view of Rashtrapati Bhavan from India Gate, so that only a dome is visible.

You can wander through the main entrances of the secretariats, now North and South blocks, where the nation's crucial decisions are made amid an ambience rendered eccentric by nesting pigeons, shuffling geriatric "tea boys" in Nehru caps and huge stacks of yellowing files.

Once atop Raisana Hill, the view presented by Rashtrapati Bhavan, now the official residence of India's president, is undeniably majestic. Lutyen's colossal Indo-Baroque rhubarb-colored sandstone masterpiece spans a 630-ft (192-meter) wide façade – larger even than Versailles, is set within 330 acres (133½ hectares) of land – which includes several formal gardens, a large military cantonment and a polo ground. Described by Lutyens as an "Englishman dressed for the climate", the building's design mixes a classical Western style with Mughal motifs, such as the delicate lattice-work *jali* screens, umbrella-like *chhatris* domes and or-nately carved stone elephants. After reaching the giant iron-grille entrance gate, you might want to explore the forecourt on foot, since although cars are permitted access around its perimeter, you can't stop and park. It's impossible to miss the soaring 145-ft (44-meter) high sandstone Jaipur Column, a gift of goodwill to the British by Maharaja Madhao Singh on the birth of New Delhi. On either side, exits pass smartly attired guardsmen and giant stone elephant portals.

Rashtrapati, residence of the Indian President

Visitors can visit the palace when the president is out of town, but it must be arranged through the Tourist Office or your country's mission well in advance.

The keys of Rashtrapati Bhavan changed hands over four decades ago, but much of the pomp and grandeur remains. At the height of the British Raj, an army of 2,000 servants was employed to keep the Viceroy's Palace pristine, including 50 whose task was simply to keep the crows off the velvet lawns and 20 to do the daily flower-arrangements – all housed in a township of their own behind the palace. Old habits obviously die hard, since many of their grown-up children do the same tasks today, and servants still use bicycles to get from one wing to another.

The adjacent **Mughal Gardens** with their perfect blossoms, tinkling fountains and immaculate lawns are a must if you are in Delhi between February and March, the only time they are open to the public. Close to the gardens on Church Road is the Cathedral Church of the Redemption, once regularly patronized by the last viceroy, Lord Louis Mountbatten and his wife Edwina.

It's a short taxi ride to the domed circular **Sansad Bhavan**, (Parliament House), designed by Baker and denounced by an embittered Lutyens as so elaborate "neither God nor Michelangelo could make sense of it". Baker playfully called it his "merry-go-round". It was created to house the Chamber of Princes, the Council of State and the Legislative Assembly. It now houses the Rajya Sabha (Council of States) and the Lok Sabha (House of the People). It's quite easy to arrange to watch India's political turbines in action – sessions are quite often, in *Times of India* parlance, uproarious, and when tempers run high, MPs have been known to throw their shoes in fury. Contact your embassy or the Tourist Office to get a pass.

Jantar Mantar Observatory built in 1724

Drive up **Sansad Marg** (Parliament Street), stopping at the **Jantar Mantar**, and pay off your driver. Tucked away in the middle of New Delhi, this intriguing astronomical observatory was built in 1724 by Maharaja Jai Singh II of Jaipur, a brilliant Hindu ruler whose obsession for the stars inspired him to pore over ancient texts, to ponder the calculations of Euclid and Ptolemy, and to poke holes in contemporary European theories. He went on to revise the Indian lunar calendar and astrological tables for the Mughal emperor Muhammad Shah and to provide him with this on-site observatory. Five similar projects are scattered across India, the most famous of which can be seen in Jaipur. The huge **sundial** is said to be accurate within two seconds. The other five instruments were designed to calculate the position of the sun, planets and stars as well as predict eclipses. It's set in pretty gardens full of cat-napping locals and palm-reading astrologers, and open from sunrise until 10 p.m. daily.

At the end of Sansad Marg, you'll come to the city's commercial heart, **Connaught Place**, a decaying amphitheater of paint-splintered arcades linked by Palladian arches that was built in 1920 and named after King George V's uncle. It helps to get your bearings once you know that eight radial avenues converge in the inner Central Park, and that the inner circle is Connaught Place, with its blocks numbered clockwise from A-F, while the outer circle is known as the Circus, numbered G-N.

Early colonials thought it compared favorably to Bath and Cheltenham: today it is is hung with *tatties*, or giant rattan curtains which shield shops from sun and rain and its pavements are covered with blood-like betel stains spat from pedestrians. It hums with freewheeling enterprise, always busy with prowling hawkers who sell everything from piles of books to peacock feathers. Vendors set up rickety stands on which they arrange spiced tidbits in little pyramids, deftly tossed together to the customer's taste and served on leafplates. In the summer heat, refrigerated water is ladled out at 50 paise a glass from huge steel box contraptions which have been ingeniously welded atop a bicycle complete with an attached umbrella. At every step, wares are laid out on the pavement, and traders try to entice passers-by into their shops. It's fun to wander at will on foot – stopping to peer at dusty façades, browse in stylish emporiums or simply observe the street life.

Eventually, you'll reach **Janpath**, originally called Queen's Way. At the top is **Palika Bazaar**, an underground warren of shops overflowing with goods, but reeking with unpleasant pissoir whiffs. Further ahead, you can wander along past the **Tibetan Market's** crammed row of stalls selling costume jewelry, tribal masks and pseudo-antiques. Visit the government-run **Cottage Industries Emporium**, the best all-India craft department store in Delhi.

A perfect treat, dining at the Imperial Hotel

By now you'll be feeling rather hot and sweaty. It's time to stop at the delightful 1930s-era **Imperial Hotel** on Janpath, beloved by the cream of Delhi's colonial aristocracy and restored beautifully. This is just the place to linger to recover from the noisy, sensory bombardment you've just been exposed to on the city's sidewalks. The palm-fringed garden lawn is nicest for lunch or tea, served by turbanned waiters. Service can be slow, but the flower-filled surroundings are exceptionally pleasant.

It's probably about 3 p.m. – and for your first day, this has probably been enough, so it's time to head back to the hotel for a lazy afternoon by the poolside.

On your first night, you may not be feeling up to much in the way of adventurous dining, preferring to keep things fairly simple. But on the other hand, this *is* your first night in Delhi so you might want to celebrate the occasion.

The **Bukhara** at the Maurya Sheraton's lobby level is your best choice. It's renowned for North-West Frontier fare in mock-rustic surroundings, where guests are invited to slip on aprons, eat with their fingers like baronial Mughals and watch the kitchen action through a glass screen. It doesn't take bookings after 8.30 p.m. Specialities include *Sikandari Raan*, a *tandoori* leg of lamb cooked to perfection after being marinated in rum and spices, *reshmi kabab*, minced chicken cooked over a charcoal fire, and the lentil-based *dal makhnai*. The best accompaniment to the spicy meal is a draught of Indian beer – preferably Kingfisher or Black Lable brands.

DAY 2

Mosques and moneylenders

Taxi to the Red Fort and a walking/cycle rickshaw foray through Chandni Chowk and the surrounding labyrinth of Old Delhi's bazaars to reach the Jama Masjid.

Make **Shahjahanabad**, the medieval walled city built by the Mughals, your sightseeing jaunt today. It offers a taste of the "real" India – a total contrast to Lutyen's spacious green city, a place of tangled alleys, vibrant color, pungent scents and frenetic crowds.

It's best not to do this tour on a Sunday when most of the fascinating bazaars close their shutters, and the Red Fort swarms with people. Bear in mind that Friday is the Muslim prayer day, interesting for seeing the Muslim community out in force, but sometimes impractical for visiting the **Jama Masjid**. Also you'll need sunglasses and both comfortable shoes and clothes. Women should take care not to dress skimpily in this extremely earthy, predominantly Muslim enclave.

Begin the day with a substantial breakfast at your hotel, then at about 10 a.m., hail a taxi to take you to the majestic **Red Fort**, or Lal Qila. Encircled by more than 1½ miles (2.4 km) of massive red sandstone battlements, the fort was built by Shah Jahan (ruled 1627-58), "Seizer of the World", the fifth Mughal emperor. He had decided to shift the hub of his empire from Agra to Delhi, sparking a construction boom between 1638-48 that created Delhi's seventh city – Shahjahanabad, now known less glamorously as Old Delhi.

Everything for sale including fake beards

Of all the Mughal emperors, Shah Jahan left the most sumptuous architectural legacy of magnificent fort-palaces and mosques, tombs and landscaped gardens, including the Taj Mahal. Under Shah Jahan's exacting patronage, the fine arts flourished as never before with a remarkable blend of Indian, Persian and even European influences, while at both Delhi and Agra, the marble inlay work known as *pieta dura* was at its finest. Within the royal citadel, the ceremonial pomp of court life reflected the overwhelming aura of power and decadence of the time.

Tantalizing reports of Shah Jahan's gem-studded palaces, marbled fountains, haughty princesses and gauzily-clad harem girls guarded by eunuches, phalanxes of warrior elephants, but above all his solid

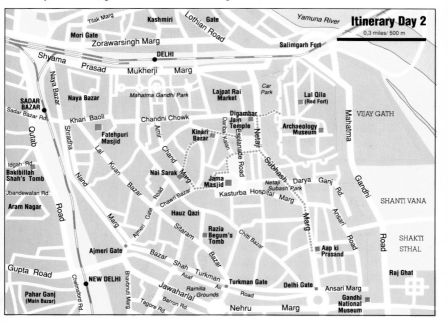

Itinerary Day 2

gold, jewel-peppered Peacock Throne, spread the Red Fort's fame.

Shah Jahan's colossal expenditure on grandiose architecture became so profligate that his son Aurangzeb, who was the last of the Great Mughals, eventually locked him up to save the dynasty from financial ruin. The Red Fort, once considered a symbol of monumental wealth, now has a desolate plundered look: all its precious gems and gilt were plucked bare in the aftermath of the 1857 mutiny.

Leave your driver waiting in the car park for you to return several hours later. Buy your Rs2 entrance ticket outside the fort entrance – taking no notice of the clamorous touts enticing you to buy fake moustaches, snake-rattlers or (inexplicably) horse whips.

Hold on to your ticket because you'll need to present it again at the inner sanctum.

Entry is through the massive **Lahore Gate**, so named because it faces Lahore in what is now Pakistan. This leads you into a vaulted shopping arcade known as **Chatta Chowk**, where royal ladies would inspect the latest creations of court goldsmiths, jewelers and weavers. Today it is full of frantically gesticulating touts, and shops selling rather tawdry "antiques", jewelry and Mughal-style miniatures – worth a browse on your return. At the end of this is the two-storied **Nakkar Khana**, (royal drum-house) the official gateway to the inner court, where court musicians would announce important visitors with deafening cymbals, trumpets and drum rolls.

The Victorian army barracks you see here were built by the British after they recaptured Delhi following the 1857 mutiny, having packed off the last Mughal emperor, the blind and feeble Bahadur Shah in disgrace to Burma. The sight of mutilated European women and children so incensed British commanders that they seriously debated totally razing both the Red Fort and the Jama Masjid to the ground.

In the end, 80 percent of the Red Fort's buildings were demolished to make way for a British military cantonment now used by the Indian Army.

Ahead is the colonaded **Diwan-i-Am** (hall of public audience), which functioned as an impromptu law court where any commoner had the right to come and plead their case before the emperor, who gazed down from an ornate palanquined throne.

Diwan-I-Am or the Hall of Public Audience

Although it looks sparse today, imagine its former grandeur when each pillar was coated with white marble, inlaid *pieta dura* and stucco gold work — and draped with rich tapestries, silk curtains and canopies.

Where the lawns are today was a huge courtyard, covered by a huge canopy, where petitioners, court officials and spectators would assemble as the emperor presided over routine government matters. The court hangman and his forty henchmen stood by, with axes and whips, ready to carry out any royal sentence promptly.

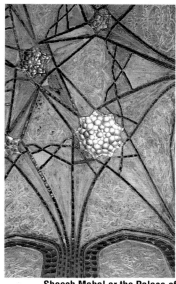

Sheesh Mahal or the Palace of Mirrors

Beyond lies the palace complex set in a large pavilioned garden through which ran an ingenious system of lotus-shaped ponds, cascading fountains and silver-plated water channels that Shah Jahan named Naher-i-Bahist, or "stream of paradise," which have sadly fallen into disrepair.

To the far right is **Mumtaz Mahal**, now a museum open from 9

Moti Masjid, the private mosque built by Emperor Aurengzeb

a.m. to 5 p.m. Close to it is **Rang Mahal**, once an elaborately painted royal harem, where Shah Jahan would retreat for sybaritic meals while musicians and beautiful dancers performed for his pleasure.

Contemporary accounts belie the story of an emperor faithful unto death to his beautiful Mumtaz Mahal, who inspired him to build the Taj Mahal. During the latter part of his reign in Delhi, Shah Jahan fell seriously ill – so, the gossip mill said, because he consumed too many over-stringent aphrodisiacs.

Moving left, you'll pass through Shah Jahan's former trio of private apartments known collectively as the **Khas Mahal**.

The palace's citadel was the adjoining **Diwan-i-Khas** (hall of private audience), where the emperor received his most important visitors while seated on his priceless Peacock Throne. Above the entrance, he inscribed: "If there is paradise on earth, it is this, it is this". Less blissfully, it was here that Muhammad Shah surrendered to the invading Persian king Nadir Shah in 1739, who went on to slaughter more than 30,000 residents of Delhi, and returned home with 1,000 elephants, 7,000 horses and 10,000 camels laden with Mughal booty, including the Peacock Throne, which was later broken up. Only fragments still remain in Iran.

Close by are the royal *hamams* (baths) where royal parties took hot saunas and steam baths, then plunged into rose-infused pools decorated with marble-inlaid floors. Behind a grand brass door lies Aurangzeb's **Moti Masjid**, or Pearl Mosque, was built for his own private worship in 1622, still quite impressive despite losing its original gilded copper domes during the mutiny.

It's worth returning one night of your stay for the excellent sound and light show dramatizing the fort's history held (in English) at 8.30 p.m. - 9.30 p.m. within the central courtyard. Bring mosquito repellent (and a rug in winter).

Directly opposite the Red Fort sprawls **Chandi Chowk** or "Moonlit Crossing", an arterial row of bustling bazaars laid out by Shah Jahan's daughter, Jehanara Begum, in 1648, with a central canal flanked by merchants and noblemen's mansions. The canal was filled in by tarmac long ago – and the street is clogged with exhaust-spewing auto-rickshaws, but otherwise you'd swear that nothing had altered substantially for centuries.

Although residents know its maze of narrow alleys like an intimate secret, newcomers often get lost quite happily for hours, riveted by its explosive streetlife, wafting scents and bizarre sights. Take any direction and you'll find yourself surrounded by an incredible variety of human and animal life. It's best to explore this area in a mood to wander at whim, jumping on a cycle-rickshaw when you feel tired or need to be whisked out of the maze. Pavement ear-cleaners and

The unique hospital for birds

teeth-quacks ply their trade. Squads of *burqa*-clad women move like shiny black shadows into narrow secret lanes. Sure-footed coolies weave in and out like human oxen. Indolent *paan*-chewing merchants cast bored glances from shops selling brass utensils or ready-made wedding turbans, or cages of squawking chickens. Wobbling rickshaws pull wooden cages of giggling kohl-eyed school-children. Ash-smeared ascetics trudge through with tridents and begging bowls.

From the Red Fort, cross on foot to the 17th-century **Digambar Jain Temple** directly opposite. It's better known by visitors for its **Bird Hospital**, where hundreds of sick birds are administered splints and medicine, and even ceremonial cremations on the Yamuna river if they fail to pull through. Non-vegetarian birds, like vultures, are considered spiritually unclean and treated only as out-patients.

Visitors are welcome, and donations help feed the birds. It's certainly an improvement on Kabutar Market, just 100 yards (100 meters) up on Netaji Subhash Marg where hundreds of birds hunch miserably together in cages awaiting buyers. Anyone for a Rs1,000 Hindi-speaking myna bird?

From here, let your feet wander. You'll see street photographers huddling behind Victorian cameras to immortalize clients against surrealistic fake landscapes. Marigolds are woven into sweet-scented garlands. Boys try to sell goldfish in whiskey bottles.

Pass **Esplanade Road**, and the next main alley on the left will be **Dariba Kalan** (the street of the incomparable pearl). This glittering stretch specializes in weight-priced gold and silver, jewelry and money-lenders and dates back to the time of Shah Jahan. Wizened shop-keepers sit cross-legged on giant white cushions, weighing gold on brass weighing scales, while displaying their jewelry in glass cases. Dozens of artisans work hunched over small lamps using tools and methods that have changed little in three centuries.

There used to be a gateway here, and when Nadir Shah invaded Delhi, it came to be known as "Bloody Gate" because this is where the bulk of the soldiers came to pillage and slaughter. Hundreds of bodies were said to have been beheaded and piled up here. You'll see plenty of bridal jewelry displayed, and gain some insights into the Indian mania for gold.

On the first alley on your right, you'll find **Kinari Bazaar** (braid-shop street), easily the most colorful place in Old Delhi.

Shops overflow with wedding garb, tinsel, gold lamè groom's turbans, huge rosettes for the traditional white-horse and currency-note garlands. The street is also a thermometer of each up-coming festival, selling *papier mâché* masks of favorite gods and elaborate props such as Krishna's cupid bows and arrows, fake swords and scabbards. Not surprisingly, festivals are celebrated in this part of town with unabashed delirium.

At this stage you may be feeling rather fractious, side-stepping speeding rickshaws, clumsy cows and bubbling vats of *ghee*, so climb aboard a cycle rickshaw – it's exactly the right pace, and enables you to see far more with-

Chandni Chowk is now one of the busiest markets

out constantly glancing behind or beneath you. Ask your helmsman to take you through **Nai Sarak** (New Street) to the **Jama Masjid mosque**. In Hindi, this goes something like: "*Aap mujhe Nai Sarak ki teraf se Jama Masjid le cheliye.*" Rs5 is quite enough. Nai Sarak is a general purpose street, selling an incredible volume of wholesale college textbooks, and every conceivable type of stationary. As you are whisked to the end of Nai Sarak, you'll enter **Chawri Bazaar**, Delhi's most extensive fake antique mart, full of workshops churning out brass statues and carved ivory.

From here it's impossible to miss the tapering minarets and sheer grandeur of the Jama Masjid, India's largest mosque. Built predominantly in red sandstone and white marble, and adorned with Mughal inlay. It was commissioned by Shah Jahan in 1644, but finished by his son, Aurangzeb, 16 years later. It's the epicenter of Delhi's Muslim community – you'll notice black flags mourning the death of Muslims in communal violence – and on Fridays and Islamic festivals, thousands of white-capped devotees prostrate themselves in the mosque, which can hold up to 20,000 people. There are three main gateways, each approached by steep flights of stairs. During the Mughal era, the emperor would ride in splendid procession through the magnificent eastern gateway to attend Friday prayers.

Within the **central courtyard** is a small marble crypt which contains various treasures – an single spiky red hair allegedly plucked from the Prophet's beard and now kept in a glass vial, the imprint of his foot at Mecca and two ancient Korans written on deer skin in

Kufic script by the relatives of the Prophet. A small booth at the entrance sells tickets to the 150-ft (46-meter) high **South Minaret**, where a 122-step climb earns you one of the best views across the old city. Women must be accompanied by "responsible family members" – a rule imposed after several incidents of molestation up in the tower.

By now you'll be quite exhausted and in dire need of refreshments. Once you've negotiated your way back to the Red Fort car park in a cycle-rickshaw, stop at **Aap ki Prasand** on Netaji Subhas Marg opposite Golcha Cinema for a glass of delicious (safely boiled and filtered!) iced mint tea in air-conditioned comfort. This is Delhi's premier outlet for **fine teas**, perfect for buying as gift-wrapped presents. The cost of hiring a taxi for the morning should come to about Rs100, plus Rs20 tip. Back at the hotel, you'll probably want a wash and a change of clothes, as well as a late snack. It's been a long, hot morning, so spend the afternoon relaxing.

Enjoy dinner in civilized, if subdued surroundings – a welcome contrast to the old city's bustling energy – at the Taj Mahal Hotel's

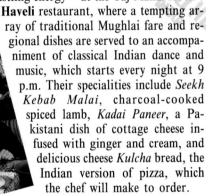

Royal dining at the Taj Mahal Hotel

Haveli restaurant, where a tempting array of traditional Mughlai fare and regional dishes are served to an accompaniment of classical Indian dance and music, which starts every night at 9 p.m. Their specialities include *Seekh Kebab Malai*, charcoal-cooked spiced lamb, *Kadai Paneer*, a Pakistani dish of cottage cheese infused with ginger and cream, and delicious cheese *Kulcha* bread, the Indian version of pizza, which the chef will make to order.

DAY 3

Time-worn tombs

A morning excursion out to Qutb Minar and Hauz Khas crafts village, lunch at Hyatt Regency, Safdarjang's Tomb and Indira Gandhi Museum, dinner at President Hotel.

One of Delhi's most famous landmarks, the **Qutb Minar**, is best visited in the tranquil cool of early morning to avoid tourists and irritating touts. Set out at about 8 a.m. Hiring a taxi for the day will come to about Rs200 in total.

The Qutb Minar is situated 0.6 miles (10 km) south of New

Delhi. This intricately-carved five-storey red sandstone minaret was the Empire State Building of ancient India. At 278-feet (72½-meters) high it's still the country's tallest man-made tower.

It was begun in AD 1199 by India's "Spartacus" – Qutb-ud-din-Aibak, a former Turki slave who rose in rank to become the first Muslim Sultan of Delhi – and was finally completed by his son-in-law and successor, Iltumish almost three decades later. The tower celebrated Aibak's victory over the last Hindu king in Delhi – and also had a dual purpose as a minaret for the muezzin to call the faithful to prayer. He built the tower to "cast the shadow of God over the east and the west", and it set the stage for just over six centuries of complete Muslim dominance of the city until British troops routed the last Mughal emperor in 1857.

Although an earthquake shattered the topmost cupola in 1803, Aibak's needle-shaped tower remains remarkably well-preserved. It's a masterpiece of design and perfect proportion, its fluted walls adorned with carvings of almost honeycomb delicacy, each tier encircled by bands of pointed stars and lotus-like curves, and enlivened by marble-inlays. Deeply-incised verses from the Koran spirals ever-larger the higher up the tower you look, so that even at the very

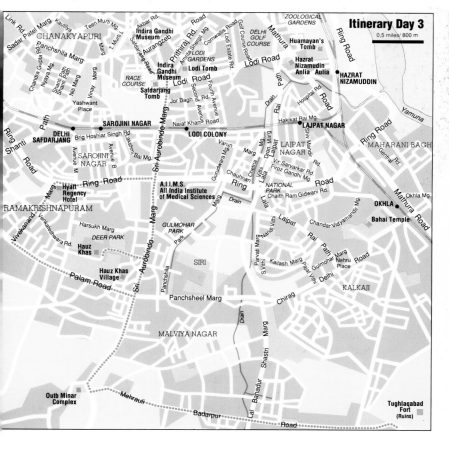

top, the magnified calligraphy allows easy visibility from the ground.

Early colonials thought it splendidly picturesque, standing as it did among hyena-infested wilds, and used its cupola as a surreptitious picnic spot.

Due to several gruesome accidents, not to mention suicidal leaps, the tower's stairway is now off-limits to visitors – which is a great pity, since its top balconies offer spectacular views.

Within the Qutb complex lies another of Aibak's achievements: India's first mosque, the **Quwwat-ul-Islam Masjid**, or the "Might of Islam" mosque, constructed from the decorative spoils of 27 demolished Hindu temples – the figures of gods and goddesses which the Muslims found offensive were defaced and turned face down. The central gateway, with its five-arched fretted *maqsura* (screen) etched with ornamental Arabic script is especially impressive.

Within the courtyard is a fourth-century Iron Pillar, apparently built as a tribute to Lord Vishnu by Hindu Tomar Rajputs, and made

15th-century Iron Pillar

of such pure iron that it has never rusted. According to lore, if you can stand back against the pillar and clasp your hands around its width, your wish will be granted. The translation of its Sanskrit inscriptions can be seen on the right hand side of the mosque near the wall.

Walking out into the gardens, see also the richly carved early 13th-century tomb of Aibak's son-in-law and successor, Iltumish, who extended the Sultanate power base in Delhi. Also, at a distance away, the vast base and unfurnished 89-ft (27-meter) high tower Alai Minar, intended to rival the Qutb Minar. It was built by Alu-ud-Din Khaljis (1296-1316), the next Muslim Sultan and architect of Delhi's second city of Siri.

On your way out of the complex, retrace your footsteps to the Qutb Minar and walk through the magnificent **Alai Darwaza**, the south entrance to the mosque precinct, built by Alu-ud-Din Khaljis in 1310. Close by is the tomb of Iman Zamin, who died in 1537 and was honored as a saint. Lastly, see the remnants of Alu-ud-Din Khaljis *madrasa*, or college for Islamic studies, and his own tomb on the way out.

The area surrounding the Qutb complex is littered with crumbling walls and ruined dwellings that are fascinating for historians, but perhaps rather too scattered and time-consuming to seek out for a casual visitor.

Among these are the 11th-century ruins of **Lal Kot**, Delhi's first city, and the 19th-century **Metcalfe's Folly** – an early 17th century domed tomb of Muhammad Quli Khan that was converted into a quirky retreat by Sir Thomas Metcalfe, the East India Company's Agent to the Mughal Court. You can find it by walking to the right of the car park, then left past the rest house until you see it ahead on a hillock.

Driving back into Delhi along the arterial Sri Aurobindo Marg once more, turn into **Hauz Khas Village**. It's easy to find if you turn left at Sri Aurobindo Market, and continue down a leafy lane through the Deer Park's huge green lung.

Enterprising young fashion designers have transformed this into a mushrooming showcase for ethnic chic, with about 20 shops tucked into white-washed old buildings – much to the capitalist delight of the local village folk hiring out their family homes. It has a very rustic atmosphere, full of grazing cows, kohl-eyed urchins and turbanned old men smoking *hookah* pipes. Bianca Jagger gave it her stamp of approval when she purchased an outfit or two on her recent visit. (See the Shopping section in this book for information on best buys at specific shops.)

At the end of the village's dirt track, you'll see picturesque ruins ahead, which overlook an **ancient reservoir** dug by Alu-ud-Din Khaljis for the inhabitants of Siri, the second city of Delhi. Today the tank is just a dust-bowl flanked by an imposing double-storied colonade of a "madrasa" or college. Nearby lies the tomb of Feroz Shah Tughlaq, who founded another of Delhi's many cities, Feroz Shah Kotla, just to the south of the Red Fort. He died in 1388.

It has been a long, rather tiring morning, so head for the nearby

Old village of Hauz Khas is now in ethnic chic

Hyatt Regency hotel, pay off your driver and treat yourself to their excellent lunch buffet (12.30 p.m.-3 p.m.) in the leafy cool of the basement coffee shop.

The next taxi stop is **Safdarjang's Tomb**. As you continue back along Sri Aurobindo Marg, you'll notice the dusty expanse of Safdarjang Airport on your left, where flying enthusiasts test out their skills. This was where Indira Gandhi's son, Sanjay, crashed his light aircraft in June 1980. At the end of Lodhi Road, Safdarjang's Tomb (1753-74) looms behind a grand entrance, the last of the great garden tombs constructed by the waning Mughals. It was built for the Nawab of Oudh, statesman and general to Mughal Emperor Ahmad Shah. Set within a well-tended garden it is an oasis of wistful charm and peace.

Further along, visit the **Indira Gandhi Memorial** at 1 Safdarjang Road, a must for those interested in modern Indian history. The charismatic daughter of India's first prime minister, Jawaharlal Nehru, Indira Gandhi governed India for almost two decades until she was assassinated by her own Sikh bodyguards on 31 October 1984 as she strolled across her garden. Both revered and villified for her autocratic style, "Mrs G" was often accused of capitalizing on the cult of the Hindu mother-goddess, especially with her election slogan, "India is Indira and Indira is India." Nevertheless, she won a permanent place in the nation's heart, as is evidenced by the hundreds of Indians who file through here daily on a sort of pilgrimage. Her simply-furnished bungalow displays her favorite possessions, everything preserved just as it was.

In the foyer, a well-documented collection of archive photographs makes fascinating viewing. Her recorded voice wafts eerily after visitors along the garden path, and at the site where she fell, her bloodstains have been chemically preserved and covered with glass.

It's late afternoon, so you'll want to relax back at your hotel now, perhaps spending the afternoon at the hotel pool, before going out to dinner at the **Tandoor**, at the less than salubrious Hotel President, on Asaf Ali Road, a seedy, murkily-lit quarter of old Delhi. Don't be put off, for here is found excellent, very reasonably-priced North-Indian food and *tandoori* specialities that have earned a following among locals, diplomats and tourists alike.

Especially good to try are the varieties of garlic and yogurt-tenderized chicken *kebabs*, which you can see chefs skewering and plunging into red-hot clay tandoor ovens from behind a glass partition, perfect when accompanied by *roomali roti*, which the chefs toss and twirl high in the air to stretch it to transparent thinness. Cross-legged musicians fingering the *sitar* provide soothing, melodic background music.

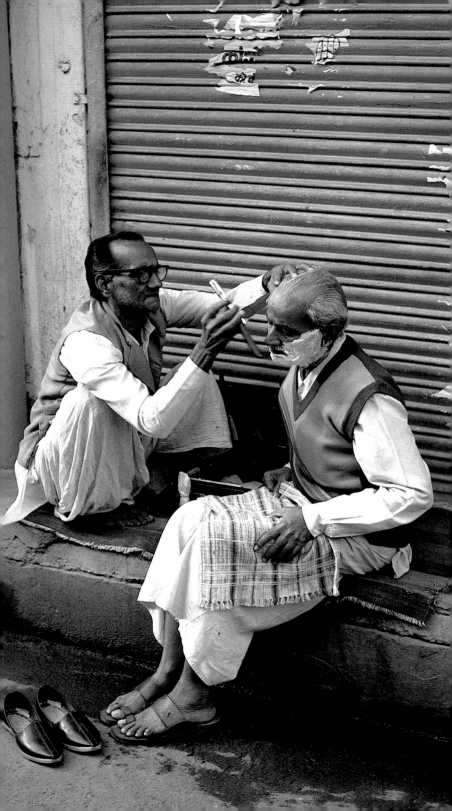

These half-day itineraries are grouped and designed according to theme. While they are quite detailed and specific, you're bound to make new discoveries of your own along the way.

A.M. Itineraries

1. Ruins, rattlesnakes and rose petals

The ruins of Purana Qila; Delhi Zoo; Crafts Museum to see artisans at work; Humayan's Tomb and a stroll through the medieval Sufi village of Nizamuddin, lunch at Dasaprakash restaurant in the Hotel Ambassador. The morning can be extended into a day by lunching before visiting Humayan's Tomb and Nizamuddin.

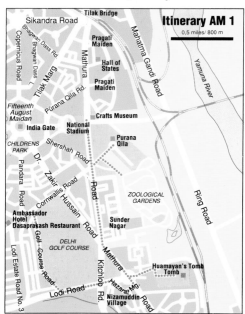

Start your day around 9 a.m. with a taxi-ride to **Purana Qila**, whose peaceful peacock-filled ruins tower above the green parkland of Delhi Zoo. Archaeologists have found artefacts here that suggest that the site beneath Purana Qila may well have been

Purana Qila or Old Fort

Indraprastha, a legendary city that was described in the Hindu epic, the *Mahabharata*, as the abode of Lord Indra, the Hindu god of rain and thunder. Excavations on the southern side of Purana Qila reveal stratified levels which date back to 1,200 BC and seem to give substance to the myth.

In 1533, the second Mughal Emperor, Humayan, laid the first foundation stone for Delhi's sixth city, which he christened Dinpanah (shelter of faith). At the time of his succession, Humayan was 23 years old, a natural recluse who lacked the military skills and acumen required to run the new empire.

He preferred to study languages, mathematics, philosophy and astronomy, and was also fond of illustrated manuscripts and opium. His plans to study were interrupted by the invasion of a brilliant Afghan commoner, Sher Shah Suri, who captured Delhi and slaughtered 8,000 Mughal soldiers. Young Humayan escaped certain death by floating across the Yamuna River on an inflated animal skin, using the Koh-i-noor diamond to bribe his way out to Persia in safety. The usurper was able to add several impressive monuments to the city he renamed Shergarh, before Humayan reclaimed his throne with a vengeance in 1555. However, he had little time to savor his return to power, for only a few months later he died after stumbling down the stairs of his library in his haste to attend the muezzin's call to prayer.

Enter the fort by the southern gate, or **Lal Darwaza**, to find the **Sher Mandal**, Humayan's two-storied octagonal library tower where his fateful fall took place. Also see Sher Shah Suri's **Qal'a-i-Kuhna**

Library and Observatory tower of Emperor Humayan

Masjid (old fort mosque), with its five arches, decorated prayer chambers and marble-inlaid sandstone. There's an interesting on-site museum housing a collection of archaeological finds that is open from 8 a.m. to 6.30 p.m. daily.

In September 1947, amid the ugly holocaust of partition, more than half a million Muslim refugees assembled among these ruins (and Humayan's Tomb) to wait in relative safety for transportation to newly-created Pakistan. An extract from *Freedom at Midnight* by Larry Collins and Dominique Lapierre sets the scene: "So terrified were those wretches by the thought of leaving their protective walls that they refused to venture out even to bury their dead. Instead they threw them from the ramparts to the jackals. Initially, the Purana Qila had two water taps for 25,000 people. Despite the growing filth, the refugees refused to clean their latrines...and at the height of Delhi's troubles, the Emergency Committee had to send a hundred Hindu sweepers under armed guard into the fort to perform the chores its Muslim inmates refused to carry out."

Right beside the Purana Qila gateway you'll find the entrance to the **Delhi Zoo**, the largest and most important in India. A wander through its landscaped gardens proves a good introduction to the animals of India's jungles. A vast array of wildlife live here in near-natural surroundings, including several rare white tigers from Rewa, Assamese one-horned rhinoceroses, Asiatic lions from Gujarat, Himalayan bears, elephants, deer, monkeys and many other creatures. During autumn, a large number of migratory birds flock to the zoo's man-made lake. Mid-summer is not a good time to visit. The zoo is open from 9 a.m. except Fridays.

As you walk back onto Mathura Road, you'll see the **ruined archway** of a Shergarh gate across the road – with plenty of ancient stairwells to clamber up and tamarind trees to sit under. Enough remains to see that the Afghan warlord had a passion for robust, mosaic-studded architecture. Next to it is the 16th- century **Khairu'l-Manazi Masjid** (the most auspicious mosque), built for the Emperor Akbar's power-wielding wet nurse, the dowager Maham Anga, who became head of his harem and had her son promoted to an army general. **Sundar Nagar market** (see Shopping section) lies further along Mathura Road.

By now, you'll have seen the vast utopian-style architecture of **Pragati Maidan**, 330 ft (100 meter) down Mathura Road, a showground that comes to life throughout the year with fairs and exhibitions. Don't miss a visit to its superb **Crafts Museum** – an essential stop if you are interested in India's cultural and village life. (It's located in the far right-hand corner of the complex, closest to Purana Qila). On display is an excellent collection of rare icons, tribal folk deities, temple lamps, wood carvings, intriguing masks and Indian textiles. The adjoining court-yard houses beautiful antique vessels.

Close by, an all-India village of 15 traditional hut dwellings has been painstakingly recreated – each hut typical of an area in India and authentically decorated inside and out. Some are smothered in the surprisingly pleasantly-textured "protective" wall-covering of mixed dried cow dung and urine – an ancient practice to ward off snakes and harness the "generative energy" of the cow, a creature sacred to Hindus. This

A taste of rural India at the Crafts Museum

base is ornamented with rice-powder or *kolam* design, life-style fresco paintings or studded mirrors.

In another courtyard, rotating shifts of craftsmen and artists create traditional fabrics, puppets, terracotta pots, brass deities,

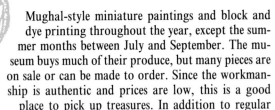

Mughal-style miniature paintings and block and dye printing throughout the year, except the summer months between July and September. The museum buys much of their produce, but many pieces are on sale or can be made to order. Since the workmanship is authentic and prices are low, this is a good place to pick up treasures. In addition to regular film shows and lectures, the workshops welcome anyone who is keen to try their hand at being a village artisan. The museum is open from 9.30 a.m. to 6 p.m., including Sundays, but is closed on national holidays.

Emerging from the Craft Museum, hail a taxi for a five-minute ride to **Humayan's Tomb**, located at the crossroads of Mathura and Lodhi roads. It's the rather awe-inspiring precursor to the Taj Mahal – the first Mughal garden tomb.

Visitors are immediately struck by the tomb's resemblance to its more famous cousin – with its four grand gateways, octagonal base-

plan, soaring niche-shaped arches, lofty double domes and the symmetrical garden with its central canal. Made of buff-colored sandstone, beautifully inlaid with black and white marble, it was built during 1555-69 by the Mughal Emperor Humayan's senior widow, Haji Begum, nine years after the emperor's death. Her tomb lies here as well, along with that of

Hukka, a gentle smoke on a quiet evening   Dara Sikoh, Shah Jahan's favorite son, and the Mughal emperors, Farruk-siyar (ruled 1713-19) and Alamgir II (ruled 1754-9). It was here that the last of the Mughals, Bahadur Shah, hid himself in the tomb of his ancestor, then gave himself up to the British – his family tragedy continued when his two sons were killed here in a shoot-out by the British vigilante officer, Captain Hodson.

Within the palm-dotted gardens are a cluster of 16th-century Mughal tombs, most of them belonging to court nobles, although in the southeast corner, a small tomb apparently belongs to Humayan's favorite barber.

Right next to Humayan's Tomb is the **Sundar Nagar Government Nursery** – a peaceful leafy place dotted with Mughal ruins, a lovely place for a walk or to sit beneath a tree, even if you have no intention of emerging with cart-fulls of foliage!

Directly opposite, across the road, explore the **medieval Sufi village of Nizmuddin**, full of concentrated Muslim atmosphere. Few tourists know of this place and so hardly come this way. Here, life follows a medieval pattern, shimmering with heat, dust and flies; women live in strict *purdah*. Goats are tethered in mud-bricked courtyards. Old men with hennaed beards commiserate with each other in the shadows, while crocheted-capped merchants gossip on upturned

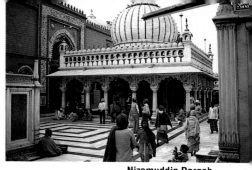

Nizamuddin Dargah

flower-pots. Stalls sell a jumble of rose petals, oil essences, *hookah* pipes, lace caps, freshly slaughtered buffalo, aromatic kebabs, Korans and luridly orange *jalebi* sweets to passing devotees. The village rose around the *dargah* (shrine) of the Sufi saint, Shaikh Nizam-ud-din Chisti (1236-1325) whose royal followers included many generations of Muslim kings.

To reach the shrine, take the winding narrow path near the police station, and ask directions if you get lost.

Nizamuddin attracts floods of pilgrims for Muslim festivals, especially **Urs**, (see Calendar of Special Events) when poetry readings, fairs and all-night performances of *qawwalis* (mystic songs) take place. Within the shrine's courtyard are several important tombs, including the court poet Amir Khusrau and Shah Jahan's daughter Jahanara, who loyally stayed with her father when he was imprisoned at Agra Fort by his father Aurangzeb.

At this stage, you'll be exhausted and famished. Take a taxi along to Dasaprakash, Delhi's best south Indian restaurant, which is tucked inside the lobby of the nearby **Hotel Ambassador**.

They offer a huge range of nutritious and popular snacks such as rice *idlies*, *uttapams* and *masala dosas* served with delicious coconut chutney, but if your appetite warrants it, order a satisfying lunch-time *thali* (served 12.30 - 3 p.m.) delivered with its colorful ring of *katoris* (little dishes), each containing a different freshly-cooked vegetable dish, with a central mound of rice and lightly-fried puffed breads. Another speciality here is freshly-squeezed unsweetened grape or *musumbi* juice.

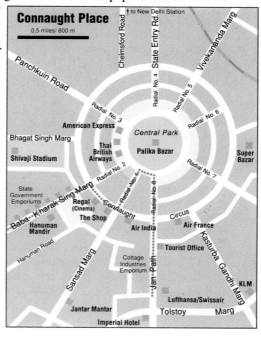

2. Monkey and markets

A serious shopping tour of Connaught Place, Janpath and Pahar Ganj. Lunch at the wacky Raj-era Gaylords restaurant, bring a good city map of Connaught Place.

Start your morning at around 10 a.m. with a peek at **Hanuman Mandir**, an action-packed little shrine located mid-way down Baba Kharak Singh Marg. Your taxi driver will know exactly where to go. This temple is dedicated to the muscle-bound, celibate monkey god Hanuman – the Hercules of Hindu mythology. He is the patron saint of wrestlers and boxers, who make sure they have a suitably bracing cold shower before coming to make their *puja* (worship) on Tuesdays, when other less athletic devotees stream in to pay their respects as well, bearing gifts of sweets and garlands.

You might see street performers here with chalk-smeared bodies, painted faces and swaying birch-switch tails doing their uncannily

Mehendi or henna-dye hand paintings

exact simian impersonations, while real monkeys up in nearby trees look on with interest.

Cross over the road to the long row of **22 government emporiums**, each specializing in the crafts of a single state. Appearances are deceptive; although they are housed in depressingly drab-looking blocks, this is the best place to fossick out some of the best handicrafts and beautiful fabrics India has to offer.

The all-round best is **Poompahar** (Tamil Nadu) for vivid *applique* lanterns, umbrellas and textiles; glazed Thanjuver pottery, elaborate south Indian temple lamps, *papier-mâché* masks and giant terracotta *ayanars*, traditionally made throughout Tamil Nadu as symbols of protection for the home and hearth. It also stocks an excellent range of beautiful bronze figures, all exquisite reproductions of original 10th to 12th-century Chola-period sculptures.

Others to seek out include **Gujari** (Gujarat) for exquisite textiles, mirror-work cushion covers and bedspreads, lacquered furniture and brightly-embroidered slippers; **Himachal Pradesh** for soft-textured woollen blankets, decorative shawls and hand-knitted socks, and delicious unsweetened apple juice; **Nagaland** for distinctive tribal rugs, textiles and ornaments; **Orissa** for aesthetic *ikat* fabric, *lunghis* and primitive *patta* paintings; and **Cauvery** (Karnataka) for fine-quality Bangalore silks and fragrant sandalwood items.

The **state emporia** are open from 10 a.m. - 6 p.m., every day except Sunday. Like all government emporia, the only drawback is its archaic system of sale. Bills are painstakingly written up in triplicate, one copy presented to one counter, another to the cashier, and the last to the collection counter.

Just opposite is the **Regal Building complex**, festooned with lurid cinema billboards of paunchy villains and voluptuously sequined heroines advertising the latest Hindi *masala* (spicy) extravaganza.

On the corner is the **Khadi Gramodyog Bhavan**, which specializes in *khadi*, the rustic, coarse, hand-woven fabric that is spun by spinning wheel, dyed, woven and printed all by hand, as opposed to so-called handloom fabrics which are mill-spun, then hand-woven. Prices are government-subsidized to promote cottage industry and the whole place is festooned with pictures of Mahatma Gandhi, who, as part of his anti-colonial Quit India campaign, urged all Indians to burn British clothes and adopt the *khadi* as a patriotic symbol of independent India.

Past Regal Cinema, look out for **Gaylords** – you'll return here for lunch – and turn around the corner onto **Parliament Sreet** (Sansad Marg) You'll find **The Shop** tucked away at No. 10, which stocks exquisite hand-printed tablecloths, napkins and fabrics – all traditional designs adapted to suit western "Laura Ashley"-style tastes. Quilts, quality leatherware, pottery, embroidered cushions and *bidri* work with its distinctive silver designs against black metal are among the treasures to buy.

Now cross over to **Palika Bazaar**, the underground rabbit warren crowded with more than 400 shops. Its cramped, stale-smelling atmosphere and confusing layout does not encourage pleasant browsing, so it's best to make a beeline for specialist shops.

Connaught Place, built for the Imperial City of Delhi

You'll find exquisite shirts and table linen embroidered with delicate *chikan* work (white embroidery on white cotton) from Lucknow at **Lal Behari Tandon**, Shop No. 20 at the end of the central hall and an excellent range of antique Rajasthani jewelry at **Jewel Mine**, Shop No. 12. **Shaw Brothers** at No. 8 stock Delhi's best range of high quality Kashmiri shawls at relatively reasonable prices – which make splendid presents, especially for older women. *Pashmina*, *shahtush* and the finely embroidered *jamawar pashmina* shawls are the ones to look for.

Shahtush shawls are the most highly prized of all – spun with fleece gathered from the throats of wild ibex goats in Ladakh and Tibet, they are so airy and feathery they can be drawn through a ring, but so warm that – it is claimed – they will cook a wrapped egg after five hours. Unlike woollen and *pashmina* shawls, *shahtush* is never dyed or embroidered, are mousy brown in color and highly sought after, costing around Rs12,000. They also have the ubiquitous Kashmiri *papier mâché* goods, Kashmiri carpets, *namadas* (brightly chain-stitched rugs made from pounded fleece) and unusual crewel-work rugs. At No. 14, **Kashmir Corner** is also worth a look for comparative prices.

Emerge from Palika Bazaar, and head for **Janpath**'s arterial row of stalls, selling mass-produced curios, costume jewelry and cheap clothes. You may want to pay another visit to the Central Cottage Industries Emporium. After you pass the intersection with Tolstoy Marg, you'll find the **Tibetan Market**, where stalls run by entrepreneurial Tibetan refugees sell a motley but interesting

The sales pitch

array of giant brass *samovars*, *kanglin* (flutes made from human shinbones), *damaru* (drums, sometimes made from human skulls) and *tankas* (religious paintings on silk). Prices tend to high and goods of inferior, mass produced quality.

After a quick refreshing cup of tea at the **Hotel Imperial**, take a taxi or auto-rickshaw to **Pahar Ganj**, just opposite New Delhi Railway Station. Disembark here, and continue down the **central Main Bazaar** on foot. This area has a reputation as a back-packer's haunt with its cheap accommodation and *dhaba*, or roadside cafés. Unexpected treasures can be unearthed here – such as lengths of antique brocade and embroidery – but it's largely an all-purpose market. Quirky items such as Victorian-style coal-heated irons, aluminium suitcases, antiquated sewing machines or huge brass kettles might interest some.

One of Delhi's most remarkable shops is tucked away at 1115 Main Bazaar, located close to the landmark Big Mosque. **R-Expo** has a staggering range of nearly a hundred essences, oils, balms, herbal soaps and shampoos, massage oils, natural henna powder and incense. Many of the perfumes are still made from specific medieval recipes, such as the unusual "oil of wet earth", which exactly recreates the scent of the monsoon. The perfumes can be gift-wrapped in lovely old bottles, and the balms enclosed in ornate sandalwood boxes – perfect as presents for friends back home.

Keep walking through the bazaar until you reach **Panchkuin Road**, Delhi's premier furniture market, liberally littered with pavement workshops. Hail an auto-rickshaw (taxis are rare along this stretch) and head for **Gaylord's** (tel: 352677) at B16 Regal Building in Connaught Place. Its plush Raj-era atmosphere is full of vintage charm, with its large ballroom-style mirrors, dangling chandeliers and aged waiters. They serve good Mughlai food and cold *lassi* drinks – just what you'll need after all that walking.

3. Spices, sweetmeats and shrines

A walk through Chandni Chowk's aromatic spice markets, with detours to Ghantewala's sweet shop, the Goddess Kali shrine and the Sisganj Gurdwara.

You can start this tour around 10 a.m., which will allow for an action-packed two hours in the old city.

Leave your taxi in the Red Fort car park, then let a cycle-rickshaw whisk you down to the 17th-century **Fatehpuri Masjid** – built by one of Shah Jahan's senior wives – at the end of Chandni Chowk – Rs 5 should be enough. Just before the mosque, you can't miss seeing a giant, garish hoarding advertising the professional services of Dr. Sablok, Delhi's most famous sexologist, whose corpulent gaze ubiquitously features in the city's newspapers, and is plastered across countless buses and street lamps.

Once outside the mosque, walk 100 yards (100 m) to your right to reach **Khari Baoli** (pronounced "curry bowly"), Delhi's maze-like wholesale spice market. Before you plunge into its frenzied oriental bedlam, look across **Church Mis-**

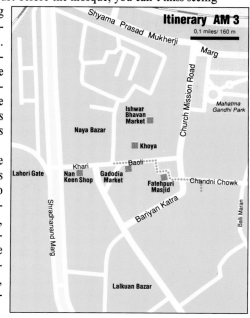

Itinerary AM 3
0,1 miles/ 160 m
Shyama Prasad Mukherji Marg
Church Mission Road
Mahatma Gandhi Park
Ishwar Bhavan Market
Naya Bazar
Khoya
Baoli
Lahori Gate
Khari Nan Keen Shop
Gadodia Market
Fatehpuri Masjid
Chandni Chowk
Shradhanand Marg
Bariyan Katra
Bali Maran
Lalkuan Bazar

Cricket match beside the Fatehpur Mosque

sion Rd to see its "slave's row" of unemployed tradesmen – painters, plasterers, electricians, plumbers, carpenters – squatting patiently with their threadbare kit bags in the hope that an employer will take them home. The fun really begins when you turn left into **Khari Baoli**.

You'll see dozens of stalls piled high with nuts, dried fruits, pods, seeds, barks, resins and wizened condiments of every conceivable kind – many mystifying even to those who pride themselves as accomplished Indian chefs.

Sculpted pyramids of powdered spices form a patchwork of primary colors and pungent scents. Tibetan mendicants in swaddled rags crouch under black umbrellas, selling noxious-smelling brown lumps, beads and potions. Heavy-lidded merchants cast bored glances amid lurid-hued jars of pickles, picking at their *paan*-stained teeth with *neem* twigs. Wiry *coolies* struggle under enormous sacks, alerting passers by to jump aside by making frantic click-click noises with their tongues and shouting "chalo, chalo" ("move, move") while-making ponderous progress.

As you walk along, look for the wrought-iron **Gadodia Market archway** on your left. As you enter, the intoxicating spice and chilli dust-infused atmosphere will have you sneezing in no time. Sixty years ago, Gadodia Market was a large *haveli* (merchant's house) – today its courtyard is lined with wholesale spice dealer's godowns.

Victorian weighing scales are put to use, while rag-tag laborers don "hair shirt" mats to protect their backs from heavy loads, or rest on sacking stuffed with dried red peppers, giggling with the camaraderie of incessant sneezing.

The next lane on your left is **Gali Batasha** (sugar meringue street), worth a detour to marvel at all the varieties of raw sugar, some resembling lumps of marble or crystal (*misri chini*), others like oozing yellow mud (*jaggery*) or white coated marbles (*prasad*). Super-thin leaves of edible silver of *vark* are also sold in bulk, destined to adorn Indian sweetmeats, but not at all recommended for those with silver fillings!

The winding, mucky little **alleys branching off Khari Baoli** are the most interesting to explore, so from here just wander where your nose leads you, from one strong spicy whiff to the next. If you want to take spices home to test out new-found culinary skills, this is the place to buy for quality and freshness, however you'll only obtain wholesale prices if you buy excessive amounts. In general, you'll recognise flame-red chilli powder, lurid yellow tumeric, khaki-colored coriander, and beige ground ginger.

Specialised alleys deal in aniseed, cardamom, caraway, melon, cucumber, poppy and pomegranate seeds, cinnamon sticks, saffron, black salt and tamarind. More exotic produce include sugar-coated rose petals, leathery strips of dried mango, puffed-up *phool-makhana*, or Indian popcorn, *neem* sticks (used as toothbrushes) and *lac*, the amber-like resin excreted by tiny forest insects and used to make industrial lacquer. Natural cosmetics are here too, in somewhat disguised forms: shiny brown *reetha* nuts and black charcoal-like *amla* seeds are both noted for promoting lustrous hair growth – and used as products in age-old Indian beauty concoctions.

At the end of Khari Baoli, intersecting Lahori Gate, is **Shradha-nand Marg**, commonly known as G.B. Road, notorious as Delhi's

Dried-spice markets of Delhi

sleazy red-light area. Hard-faced Nepali girls and heavily made-up eunuches solicit customers from their upper storey flats, full of scampering children and faded washing.

You'll soon notice something different here by the milling crowd of men, (mainly auto-rickshaw drivers) craning their necks on the other side of the street. While perfectly safe during the day, it's not wise to come here at night. Walk or take a cycle-rickshaw back down **Chandni Chowk**, looking out for the historic **Ghantewala**, or "Bell Ringer" sweet shop half way down on your right.

Founded in 1790, it once supplied sweetmeats to Mughal royalty – the recipes are just the same today. Apparently the shop got its name from a sugar-addicted royal elephant who could never pass by without ringing his bell and refusing to go further until he was offered some sweets. If you haven't tried Indian sweets, now is your chance, you can buy some for an after-lunch treat. Particularly delicious are the toffee rings called *sohan halwa*; *gulab jamun*, a Bengali sweet of fresh cheese soaked in rose sugar syrup; and the cashew-studded condensed milk concoction of *kaju-ki-barfi*.

Stop at the **Fountain Chowk**, with its landmark Victorian fountain and 1930s-era Majestic Cinema. As far back as Shah Jahan's time this site was used as a *kotwali*, which roughly translates in current lingo as a police station. Prisoners were imprisoned in barracks here, and frequently executed in public.

It was here that the dead sons and grandsons of the last Mughal Emperor, Bahadur Shah Zafar, were displayed by vengeful British troops in the aftermath of the 1857 Mutiny – fellow mutineers usually met with the more gruesome punishment of of being blown to bits from the mouth of a cannon.

Walking up to the Majestic Cinema from Chandni Chowk, look for the first alley on your right. About two-thirds the way down you'll find the **shrine** dedicated to the goddess Kali, the malevolent destroyer. Kali is usually depicted as a gorgon-like creature with beady red eyes, dripping with blood and triumphantly holding weapons, snakes and severed heads in her ten arms. Of all the Hindu deities, Kali is the most feared and hence revered most slavishly. Unlike many other Kali temples however, this particular shrine is not notorious for its daily animal sacrifice – usually goats or sheep. Instead devotees flock to make their *puja* of sweetmeats, fragrant flowers and coconuts.

From here, retrace your steps back to **Chandni Chowk**. Directly opposite is the **Sisganj Gurdwara**, one of the more important Sikh shrines in Delhi. t was built in the memory of the martyred Guru Tegh Bahadur,

Indian sweets for the sweet-toothed only

the ninth Sikh guru, who was beheaded on the site by the Mughal Emperor Aurangzeb (ruled 1618-1707) in 1675. You're welcome to step inside, but you must leave your shoes with the free baggage counter and cover your head with a cloth first – a draped handkerchief is considered quite respectable for non-Sikhs and women. Inside the complex is a *langar*, or communal kitchen, that provides free meals for up to 2,000 people each day – regardless of caste, race, religious persuasion or color. As you leave the temple you'll be given blessed offering called *karah*, of mixed wheat and *ghee* (clarified butter), which you can politely accept.

Outside, colorful stalls sell all the five "K's" each male Sikh must possess: the *kangha* or comb with which to dress one's uncut locks or *kesh*; glittering steel *kankan* bangle, utilitarian *kacha*, or boxer shorts, and the ornate ceremonial dagger, *kirpan*. They also sell brightly-colored turbans, special fly-whisks, and bright cloths which are used to reverently keep editions of the Sikh Bible, the *Guru Granth Sahib*, in pristine condition.

Right next door is the gold-topped **Sonehri Masjid**, the mosque from which the Persian king Nadir Shah stood to exhort his soldiers to carnage and slaughter.

By now you'll be quite tired and very hungry – it's time to locate your driver back at the Red Fort car park, and head back to your hotel for lunch. However the truly adventurous will enjoy making a detour to **Paratha Wallah Gully**, "The Alley of Bread Sellers", which is wedged in Chandni Chowk's lanes and a popular lunch-time spot for locals. Originally established in 1875, this historic row of cafés is run by high-caste Brahmins, employing Fagan-like urchins as adept "street chefs".

Over the decades it has catered to everyone from British administrators to jailed opposition leaders. Its fame rests on its fresh unleavened *paratha*, sprinkled with cumin, caraway, sesame seeds, or stuffed with peas, onions or potato, according to the customer's taste. While the restaurants barely conform to Western standards of cleanliness, you'll dine extremely well here on insatiable amounts of sizzling hot *parathas*, all served with rounds of freshly-cooked *subze* (spiced vegetable), banana chutney and curd for less than Rs20, including a Limca drink. No one I know has ever gotten "Delhibelly" here!

To find it, walk 109 yards (100 m) back up Chandni Chowk, keeping to the same side of the road, until you see a large Central Bank of India opposite. This is your cue to turn into a tiny lane which should lead you into the spice-smelling *cul de sac* of your search. Don't worry if you seem to be getting lost – everyone in Chandni Chowk will know how to point you in the right direction.

4. Culture backgrounder

Tour of the National Museum and Museum of Modern Art, detour to Ugrssan-ki-Baoli. Lunch at Nirula's.

You can have a late morning start and still have plenty of time for this one. The **National Museum**, located just south of Raj Path on Janpath, has a stunning collection of classical Indian sculpture and artifacts, offering a taste of the tremendous wealth and scope of India's ancient treasures.

Before you even enter the museum, you will see exquisitely executed life-size replicas of some of India's most famous finds within the courtyard of the Archaeological Survey Office headquarters to the right. See especially the **Buddhist gateway** from Sanchi, **Akbar's honeycomb throne** from Fatehpur Sikri, **Emperor Ashoka's lion-faced capital** from Somnath. A replica of Ashoka's rock edicts from Girnar lies outside the museum entrance.

Inside as you walk from wing to wing, you'll find prehistoric and Indus Valley artifacts, exquisite sculptures which once graced ancient Dravidian temples, and many central Asian antiquities.

On the ground floor, a newly-opened Bronzes Gallery displays

Sculpture Garden of the National Gallery of Modern Art

almost 100 priceless bronze statues spanning the period 5th century to the 19th century. Upstairs is a huge display of Mughal and Rajasthani miniature paintings which depict courtly life and the rigors of the battlefield. Another interesting section is devoted to the spoils netted by Sir Marc Aurel Stein as he explored the ancient Silk Route to Tibet early this century – the other half of his huge collection lies in the British Museum in London. Another is the collection of Gandharian art from the 4th century AD, unearthed from present-day Pakistan, where Alexander the Great and his army invaded before returning home. This produced a fascinating fusion of Roman-Hellenic artistic ideals – including the draped *toga* that some claim inspired the *sari* and the bare torso – and Buddhism, the emerging religion of the time.

Also of interest is a fine collection of folk, classical and tribal musical instruments in the new wing. The gallery shop sells excellent replicas of various well-known sculptural friezes and fragments at very cheap prices – nice for souvenirs or gifts.

The museum is open from 10 a.m. to 5 p.m., and it can be worth coinciding your visit with an excellent free conducted tour, since knowing more about the museum's extraordinary collection helps bring the pieces alive – and if you lose interest you can always stray. The tours are in English, and the daily schedule is as follows: 10.30 a.m., 11.30 a.m., noon, 2 p.m. and 3.30 p.m. Films about India's artistic heritage are shown every day at 2.30 p.m. and 4 p.m.

Nirula's Salad Bar

You may now be feeling rather "museumed out." But those who are still eager for more cultural appreciation can visit the **National Gallery of Modern Art**, housed in what was once Jaipur House, home for Jaipur's royals when they came to Delhi. It's located about 10 minutes walk away, just south of India Gate.

The downstairs galleries have a shifting array of temporary exhibitions, while upstairs can be seen many of the picturesque 18th-century Indian paintings produced by the famous British uncle and nephew Thomas and William Daniell, as well as canvases by well-known Indian painters of the so-called Bengali "Renaissance" of the 1930s, notably Jamini Roy and Nandalal Bose.

After the tour, as you head towards Connaught Place for lunch; keep your eyes open for other vintage **town palaces** originally used by visiting Indian princes and still very grand, dotted around India Gate. To the north is **Hyderabad House**, designed by Lutyens for the fabulously rich Nizam of Hyderabad, and **Baroda House**, now the headquarters for Northern Railways, which is open to the public. Make one last detour by driving up **Kasturba Gandhi Marg**, and taking Hailey Road on your right to find a little-visited gem called **Ugrasen-ki- Baoli** (step-well). It dates from the 14th century, when Delhi was ruled by the Muslim Tugluq dynasty; and a small mosque of the same vintage guards its steep stairs leading down to a brackish pond.

Now it's time to take some well-earned refreshments at **Nirula's**, at L-Block Connaught Place. This is Delhi's answer to a pseudo-American fast food parlor, complete with french fries, "buffalo"

Fortified Royal Palace at Tughlaqabad

burgers, thick-shakes and ersatz pizzas – great if you need a change from curries. This is the "in" place with Delhi's gum-chewing, jean-clad yuppies. The street-level ice-cream parlor provides an extra post-prandial indulgence, and proves that Indian ice-cream can be extremly delicious, if not quite up to Haagan Daaz standards.

Rhesus monkey

5. Fortress foray

A walk through rambling ruins of the magnificent fortress of Tughlaqabad, with a detour to the tombs of Balban, Jamali-Kamali and Adham Khan and the nearby Metcalfe's Folly in the vicinity of Mehrauli village. Best for a morning when you feel like escaping the city, bring a map and picnic if you wish.

This is an ideal morning for rising late, having a swim or even being completely sybaritic and be pampered with beauty treatments or a herbal oil massage at the hotel health club – both do wonders for those who need a break from Delhi's heat and dust.

Set off late, at about 10.30 a.m., and tell your driver to take you to **Tughlaqabad Fort** – his nearest landmark is the Qutb Minar, from which the eastwards Mehrauli Badarpur Road stretches through a "cowbelt" cluster of tiny villages for a further five miles (eight km) before reaching your destination, the site of Delhi's third city, on the left.

The majestic ruins of this rambling fortress have an almost biblical quality, looming above the sepia scrubland of Delhi's outskirts. Laid out on an octagonal plan, with 4 miles (6½ km) of sloping battlements studded with 13 gates, it is undeniably the most spectacular of all Delhi's ancient cities.

It was built by Ghiyas-ud-din-Tughlaq, a strict Muslim and a just administrator, (ruled 1320-5), the first of the formidable Tughlaq dynasty, who built no fewer than three cities in Delhi during the 14th century. Whether or not this fort is haunted – as the story goes – by the ghost of a vengeful saint, is a matter for speculation, but within five years of its completion it was abandoned due to a shortage of water.

Tughlaq's son, Muhammed Shah (1325-51), an Indian "Nero" renowned for his despotic ways, took advantage of the elderly king's return from a journey to carry out a treacherous plan: he constructed a special "welcome" archway that collapsed with the tread of the

57

royal retinue of elephants, crushing his father to death.

On his succession, Muhammed Shah moved away from his father's fortress and built Jahanapanah, whose fragmented walls stretch between Lal Kot and Siri.

Today, Tughlaqabad's fragmented ruins, winding medieval passages and steep ramparts enclose a peaceful wilderness inhabited only by Gujars or gypsy herdsmen, goats, monkeys and peacocks – a perfect refuge from the city's hectic bedlam, where you can explore and picnic undisturbed. To get your bearings from the main entrance, look for the remnants of the colonnaded citadel on your right, the royal palaces on your left, and the walled city ahead.

Walking back towards the carpark, the **tombs of Ghiyas-ud-Din and his clan** are reached at the end of a raised causeway, originally surrounded by water. The guardsman gives an entertaining tour and spotted history, pointing out the tomb of Tughlaq's pet dog and the dungeons where victims were thrown to rot with snakes and scorpions with particular relish.

On your way back, make a detour to **Mehrauli Village** (0.6 miles/1 km from Qutb Minar) to seek out the picturesque ruins of the **tomb and palace of Ghiyathu'd-Din Balban** (1266-86), a ruler of the Slave Dynasty. Just south lies the 16th-century tomb of Jamali Kamali, a famous poet whose real name was Shaikh Fazullah. His verses are inscribed in Persian on its walls.

Close to the Mehrauli bypass, you'll notice an incongruous looking pair of English-style towers standing atop a boulder. These once formed the entrance to a quirky country retreat built in 1844 by Sir Thomas Metcalfe, who was Resident at the Mughal Court. He converted a domed tomb into a sumptuous mansion and named it Dilkusha or "pleasing to the heart", but it came to be known as **Metcalfe's Folly**. Most of it has crumbled away, and it lies within a military compound, so it is off limits to visitors, but you can still get a glimpse of it.

At the end of Mehrauli township, closest to the Qutb Minar, you'll find **Adham Khan's two-storied octagonal tomb**, known locally as the "bhul-bhulaiyan" or "lose your way" labyrinth for its twisting maze of mysterious bat-infested passages. It is the burial place of both Adham Khan, Emperor Akbar's foster brother and his shrewd and powerful mother, Maham Anga, who began as the emperor's wet-nurse and whose mosque you have already visited opposite the Purana Qila. Between them, the perfidious mother and son attempted to stage a *coup*, beginning with executing Akbar's chief minister in his private palace quarters at Agra. The emperor, who was then just 19-years old, retaliated to this treachery by knocking Adham Khan unconscious, then had him thrown from the Agra fort ramparts. The first fall failed to kill him, so his mangled body was hauled up and thrown a second time. Akbar himself broke the news to Maham Anga, who built this tomb and died shortly afterwards. There are few visitors, except children who come to play tag in the cluster of mosques or splash in a splendid old *baoli*, or step-well, nearby.

6. Memories of the Raj

A foray north of old Delhi brings you to Civil Lines, the historic British cantonment before New Delhi was even an architectural glint in Lutyen's eye, this settlement of 19th-century bungalows remained a provincial backwater set amid the hyena-infested wilds and majestic ruins of fallen empires until 1911, when Delhi was proclaimed the new capital of British India.

This is an excursion tailor-made for Raj-era enthusiasts – and definitely not recommended for those who find the idea of traipsing through old churchyards or admiring the exteriors of historic homes very dustily dull! You'll find yourself almost completely alone, for few of these places draw many visitors. It helps to bring them to life by going well-primed on eye-witness accounts of the 1857 Mutiny, and you'll find a special mention of recommended books on our reading list.

Silver jewelry shop

The revolt of the sepoys, or British-employed native soldiers, is called the Indian Mutiny in the West but titled the "War of Independence" in modern Indian school primers. Either way, both sides spilled much blood. The year-long rebellion was sparked in Meerut, 31½ miles (50 km) away, on 10 May 1857 by protesting sepoys incited by a rumor that new bullets were being issued greased with animal fat from pigs, which are deemed unclean by Muslims, and cows, which are sacred to Hindus.

In the space of an afternoon, 47 battalions mutinied and began a bloody spree across north India. They arrived in Delhi after a day's gallop to bayonet every European in sight and to secure the reluctant support of their symbolic emperor, the 82 year-old Bahadur Shah, in their furious bid to oust the interfering *feringhi*, or foreigners.

If you have a genuine interest in discovering more about Delhi's British history, then contact Nigel Hankin, a self-styled expert who has lived in Delhi since 1947 and offers an eccentric, highly informative "Mutiny Tour". He can be reached through the British High Commission, and charges Rs400 for the morning, regardless of how many people there are, and exclusive of taxi hire.

Today, hire a taxi for the morning, which should cost about Rs150 – and an extra Rs100 if you drive out to the Coronation Memorial. Kashmiri Gate is the nearest landmark for your first stop, the 19th-century **Lothian Road Cemetery**, tucked behind a crenellated gateway beneath Lothian Bridge, a railway fly-over at the intersection with Netaji Subhash Marg. Within the overgrown garden, moss-encrusted masonry illustrate the perils faced by early British settlers' – all buried between 1808 to 1867 – premature deaths, exotic malaises and in some cases, too much port. A Celtic cross commemorates the nameless graves of Europeans killed during the Mutiny.

Continuing down Lothian Road, look for an arched ruin on a grassy traffic island – all that remains of the **British Magazine**, once fortified to store huge supplies of ammunition. It was deliberately blown up on 11 May 1857 to prevent it falling into the hands of approaching sepoys, with an explosion that could be heard as far away as Meerut. The brave British clerk who offered to light the fuse was blown to bits as well. The insignificant-looking obelisk slightly further up on a second island is the **Telegraph Memorial**. It was from this site that two Anglo-Indian signallers first alerted the rest of India to the alarming uprisings in Meerut and Delhi, sending the classic after-thought, "we are off". Across the road, on the right, you'll see the columned, green-shuttered **Old Residency**, (now the Department of Archaeology), first occupied by Sir David Ochterlony from 1803, a great eccentric who lived the life of an oriental *pasha* with his *hookah* pipes, many Indian wives and pet elephants.

Ahead lies the crescent-shaped **Raj-era mall** of antediluvian mock-Tudor shops considered very select in the 1920s, but now very seedy. A peeling sign announces the location of the "The Bengal Club" which no longer exists. The most buoyant survivor is Varma's leather shop, which proudly carries the insignia of the British crown on its portico, listing among its patrons Queen Mary, Lord Willingdon and the Lord Mayor of London. It still makes luggage to pre-war specifications – a gold mine for lovers of antique suitcases!

The Greco-colonial **St. James Church** (consecrated in 1836), stands in a tranquil graveyard across the road. It was built by the larger-than-life Col. James Skinner, the son of a Scotsman and his Rajput mistress, who founded the Indian Army's yellow-clad Skinner's Horse cavalry regiment. Inside are beautiful stained-glass windows, oak pews and fascinating plaques to a deceased *Who's Who* of 19th-century Anglo-Indian families, swarms of whom perished at the sepoys' hands. Skinner's own tomb is by the altar and his many family members were buried outside – when he died, 64 men contested his estate, claiming they were his sons. Sunday services are held in English, with the resident organist pounding out *We Plough The Fields and Scatter*. At all other times, between 8 a.m. and 5 p.m., a church attendant should be on call to let you in with a key.

Around the corner stands **Kashmiri Gate**, the last surviving double-arched entrance to old Shahjahanabad, pock-marked with musket shots and now home to bivouacking street urchins. On 14 September 1857, it witnessed desperate carnage as a 4,500-strong British garrison stormed down from the North Ridge beyond, and after six days of heavy fighting and hundreds of casualties on both sides, succeeded in wresting back Delhi from more than 20,000 mutineers. Among those who died near here was Brigadier-General John Nicholson, one of the great stoical heroes of the Mutiny, who so impressed his Indian admirers that some claimed this "Nikkul Sen" was actually a reincarnation of Brahma. The **Nicholson Cemetery**, which contains his grave, is full of Victorian pathos, located just up the road to the left, intersecting Qudsia Marg.

The leafy gardens with domed Mughal ruins to the right are known as **Qudsia Bagh**. Although they don't really merit a visit they have an interesting history – laid out in 1748 by Qudsia Begum, a beautiful nautch girl who danced her way into the heart of the Mughal Emperor Muhammad Shah to become his favorite wife and mother of the next emperor. You'll remember Muhammad Shah was the hapless fellow who watched the Persian king Nadir Shah plunder his city in 1737.

Continue down Boulevard Road until you reach the turning into Rani Jhansi Marg which winds uphill onto North Ridge, a peaceful scrubland refuge. On your right you'll see the **Mutiny Memorial**,

The old Secretariat

renamed Ajitgarh, which looks like a lopped-off Gothic cathedral spire. It marks the spot where the party of cholera-stricken, beleaguered British, Gurkha and Sikh soldiers camped out for several weeks before mounting their assault, and commemorates those who died in the attempt. Understandably, after Independence, the Indian government didn't take kindly to these sentiments, and counter-attacked by erecting a new plaque here to honor "those who rose against colonial rule and fought bravely for National Liberation." The gate is locked, but it's easy to scramble through the fence and worth it for a panoramic view across Delhi's skyline.

Further up the road on your right, is a motley-looking **Ashokan pillar**, (273-236 B.C.) patched up after being broken in many pieces, with most of its Brahmi script worn away. It was brought to Delhi by Feroz Shah Tughlaq, a Sultan of the 14th century. (See P.M. Itinerary 3).

Opposite, within the compound of the Hindu Rao Hospital, drive in to see William Fraser's colonnaded 19th-century bungalow on the left, now called **Hindu Rao's House**. Fraser was one of Delhi's early British commissioners, a swaggering Byronic figure who had a harem of seven and claimed to have killed 84 lions. His career ended in 1835 when he was shot point-blank by an enraged Muslim noble convinced he was out to seduce his beautiful sister. Ahead, on the right, look for the ruins of a 14th-century mosque and lodge that belonged to Feroz Shah Tughlug's Kuskh-i-Shikar (Hunting Palace) when this area was thick with ferocious tigers and hyenas.

Flagstaff Tower stands on the crest, slightly off the road, with a gate entrance. Terrified British *memsahibs* and children fled here on 11 May 1857, as sepoys began rampaging in Civil Lines. The lucky ones escaped to nearby Kurnaul (Karnal) in native costume or in covered palanquins, with the connivance of their servants, others were butchered with hog-spears in their bungalows.

Turn right down Rajpur Road, then left along Underhill Road's enclave of dilapidated bungalows to reach the **Oberoi Maidens Hotel** on Sham Nath Marg – a good place to rest a while over morning tea. The oldest hotel in Delhi, this *pukka* Georgian-style establishment was where Lutyens stayed while he planned New Delhi, and

St. James Church

hosted a ball for Edward, Prince of Wales, before all the Mrs Simpson business.

Several other Raj-era treasures lurk nearby, difficult to hunt down unless you are especially zealous. Closest are the **Old Secretariat**, just north of here, and the once-magnificent **Metcalfe House** not far from Delhi University at the northern end of Mahatma Gandhi Marg. Built in 1835, it was the museum-piece home of Sir Thomas Metcalfe, British Resident of the Mughal Court, who transferred all his family art treasures from England to India. Metcalfe died in this house in 1853, which was later occupied by his nephew, Sir Theophilus, Joint Magistrate and a key figure in rousing Delhi's Europeans to arms against the mutineers.

Finally, the **Coronation Memorial**, site of the 1911 Delhi Durbar, located in desolate marshland near Kingsway Camp in north Delhi and the Yamuna River, is a curiously affecting and perhaps the most forlorn relic of India's imperial past, to be found in Delhi. Empty and deserted now, this was where the dazzlingly profligate Durbar was held to crown King George V Emperor of India, an event glittering with British aristocracy, maharajahs resplendent in traditional finery, caparisoned elephants and limitless pomp. Here, the new emperor broke the news of the shift of India's imperial capital from Calcutta to this "beautiful and historic city." Never had the British believed so firmly that they ruled India by divine right. Today, all that remains is a decaying collection of marble statues of long-dead

Adham Khan's Tomb

colonial masters amid sickly tamarind trees. Most notable is the one of King George V, haphazardly patched up after being broken in five places after Independence, which Lutyens had commissioned to stand in pride of place beneath a canopied *chatris* near India Gate – now left empty as a symbol of a free India.

7. Buygones: antique and curio hunting

A zig-zagging taxi trail through old Delhi's Chawri Bazaar, with forays to south-Delhi's Sundar Nagar Market and the suburban neighborhood of Greater Kailash.

Delhi can be a gold mine for discerning collectors and impulsive would-be treasure hunters alike. The trail through the city's musty, dust-laden curio bazaars is in fact, so absorbing that it merits a special tour all to itself. Part of the excitement of antique-hunting is that you begin to find yourself in a jungle world of cobwebbed-filled rooms and dark alleys – and here you will find them in plenty.

This magical mystery tour could easily keep a real enthusiast happy all day, but take it at your own pace, until your energy (or wallet) start wearing thin. Remember, browsing will always be free even if you don't need a carved rosewood door, 10 ft (3 meters) high and almost as wide that could fill the entrance of a small cathedral, a gilded angel from Goa, a faded lithograph of a demented, long-dead Nawab, an exquisite brass door knob or a Raj-era chamber pot!

Of course it always helps to be one of those people who can walk into an antique shop, dig through centuries of dirt and pick out a priceless bronze or a rusty blade still dripping with the blood of Genghis Khan. But for those of us with less well-honed instincts, here are a few general **words of advice** before you set out.

Never trust the integrity of others, especially shifty-eyed curio salesmen, who are capable of spinning any tale under the sun to woo your rupees. They will sing the praises of a "rare, extremely antique" piece and bluster at suggestions of inflated price. A friend was once told that a convincingly-aged, brass-studded jewelry chest had belonged to a Mughal-era Muslim noblewoman, only to find a tiny "Made in Delhi, Gopal Ram & Co. Chawri Bazaar" sign moulded into its base!

The export of genuine antiques from India is strictly illegal, and any object – be it a paperweight or a pearl necklace – comes under this restriction. Like many things in India, there are often ways and means around this ban, but woe betide those who are caught trying to smuggle a 10th-century Chola bronze in their undergarments! (They will have their prized purchase confiscated and be given a severe reprimand.) Because of this restriction, most shops in Delhi specialise in "new antiques" – many less than a week old in some cases – but very realistically deceptive.

If you're doubtful about the authenticity or age of objects that you're on the verge of spending a large sum on, it is very wise to **have art objects verified at the Archaeological Survey in India,** next to the National Museum on Janpath. Gemstones and jewelry can be taken to the **Gem Jewelry Export Promotion Council**, 10th floor, Nirmal Towers, 26 Barakhamba Road, near Connaught Place, and open from 11 a.m. to 3 p.m., Monday to Tuesday. Charges are minimal and a trip makes for secure peace of mind – and reliable dealers should not object, provided you are accompanied by one of their ilk.

Start your morning late, around 10.30 a.m. and drive down for another foray to old Delhi, leaving your taxi driver to loiter at Jama Masjid for an hour or two. Directly opposite is **Pai Walan Bazaar**, which mainly deals in luridly-packaged wholesale "Cock Brand" fireworks. With each festival, giant bamboo-frame *papier mâché* idols spill out on the pavement, waiting to be stuffed with gunpowder for a pyromaniac's gleeful delight.

Pai Walan's cluster of curio shops offer a taste of what is to

Memorial of the Mutiny or Revolt of the Sepoys

come in **Chawri Bazaar**, Delhi's frenetic Portobello Road. Nowhere else in India will you find such a concentration of workshops engaged in mass-produced, high quality replicas. Away from the main thoroughfare, workshops are hidden away in dark alleys behind rickety, 17th-century carved *havelis*, or merchants' houses. If you're interested, you can ask to step inside to watch skilful artisans industriously applying an "antique finish" to cast-bronze statues, wooden carvings and paintings – a sort of rejuvenation surgery in reverse.

Since most of the items here are **specifically manufactured for wholesale export**, owners are not angling to rip customers off, so this is **a good place to buy**. Wander at will among squat Buddhas, ornate south Indian temple lamps, old medicine chests and painted horses. As you near **Nai Sarak**, shops begin to gleam with rows of brass and copper utensils, very aesthetic and eye-catching in their own right. You might be interested to know that during the 19th century, this area was notorious for its highly talented *nautch*, or courtesan dancers. With their eyelids shaded in gold leaf, and clad in gauzy silks, they would perform seductive dances for those able to afford their price. Even up until the early 1930s no fashionable gathering was complete without them, and the most glamorous were as famous as Indian starlets today.

After an hour's wandering, it's time to climb into the taxi and head for **Sundar Nagar Market**, close to the Purana Qila and Zoo – a mecca of about 30 shops of antique jewelry, artefacts and tribal art. Just about everything seems to be here – from His Master's Voice gramophones to talismanic wooden "shrivelled" heads worn as necklaces by the head-hunting Nagas of yore to pornographic Mughal miniatures. Each shop is a mini-museum and owners are happy to chat away. It takes at least an hour to poke through these fascinating shops which seems to spill out onto the pavement with a profusion of old furniture, camphor chests and decorative doors.

All are worth a browse, but particularly, look out for the following shops: **Ellora** at No. 9 specialises in elaborate silver frames and Tibetan, Himalayan and tribal art objects, including huge ornamental head-pieces studded with Ladakhi *zu*, or amber, silver, coral, turquoise and wooden prayer beads, as does the **Ladakh Art Gallery** at No. 10. **Padma Gems** at 9 A displays very exclusive and expensive jewelry creations for well-heeled locals, but mainly exports to Geneva. There are two shops run by the personable and entrepreneurial Bakhival brothers. The first, **Poonam Bakhival** at No. 5, is a collector's lair of exquisite antique silver ornaments, terracotta and stone carvings. The second is **La Boutique** at No. 20, the best shop of its kind in Delhi, with high quality antique replicas, painted wooden toys, old lithographs, postcards and paintings – all reasonably priced. Finally at No. 12, **Mittal Stores** stocks the full range of quality Indian teas, from Assam to the Nilgiris, Kashmiri saffron, pure Vanilla powder and south Indian spices – good to stock up one's kitchen with.

For some serious refreshments, drive to the nearby Oberoi Hotel and pay off your driver – about Rs150 for the morning. The poolside **Esmeralda restaurant** is a pleasant, restful haven for a lunch of light Mediterranean food. Their home-made *cassata* ice-cream is a must.

After lunch, hail a taxi to **Greater Kailash II**, about 15 minutes from here. Your goal is to locate both branches of **Mehra Antiques** run by Delhi's "antique mafia", Mehra brothers, who also have a shop in the Red Fort Arcade. Both are "godowns", every inch crammed with an overwhelming quantity of antique furniture: every kind of Rajasthani carved wood, brass-studded bedsteads, old Corinthian-style columns, antique bronze platters and giant chunks of fallen temples. The first Mehra's is at **E 328, Street 4,** and the second, at **M-Block Market**. The important thing for your driver to know when searching for the latter is, that it should not be confused with M-Block Market of Greater Kailash I.

After all this you'll be rather "antiqued-out" but hopefully you'll have made some delightful purchases and can retire for the afternoon. If you're still interested in seeking out other specialist shops, refer to the *Shopping* section of this book.

While in Greater Kailash, you might be interested in looking for a nearby architectural "antique": the

Cheap literature and ver-
million color for makeup

Khirki Masjid, which should be well known to any taxi driver in the suburb. Rarely visited, this beautiful 14th-century mosque is buttressed with massive monolithic pillars and offers a splendid oasis of atmospheric charm set in its peaceful garden. It was built by Khan-i-Jahan Jumna Shah, the son of Feroz Tughlaq's powerful minister, Khan-i-Jahan Tilangani.

8. Sultanpur Bird Sanctuary

Visit a marshland oasis of peaceful nature.
Bird lovers will enjoy Sultanpur in neighboring Haryana, 29½ miles (47 km) away. Rise at dawn for this excursion and you can be back in Delhi for lunch. The best season to go is between **November and February**, when the sanctuary's small lake attracts lots of migratory birds such as the Greater Flamingo, Bar-headed and Brahminy ducks from Tibet. Hire a taxi with an All India Tourist Permit for the drive, 50 minutes each way, and should cost about Rs350 return. **Gurgaon** is the nearest town, 5½ miles (9 km) away. Take a picnic, and good walking shoes for marshland strolls.

P.M. Itineraries

9. Away from the crowds

A South-Indian lunch; the Rail Museum, Tibet House and the Lodhi Gardens.

This is a good tour when you need a very relaxed afternoon away from the city's dust and bustle.

Those with a newly-acquired enthusiasm for the almost exclusively vegetarian south Indian cuisine will enjoy today's choice of venue for lunch. **Sagar Restaurant**, (tel: 617832) at 18 Defence Colony market, has no pretensions to glamor – its shabby but clean interior is decorated with garish Hindu calenders, but this is where you'll find the city's most delicious, authentic and freshly-prepared south Indian food. Look around the well-crammed room, and you'll see plenty of darker-skinned, Dravidian-featured Southerners tucking in with relish – always a good sign. You can order *thali*, filled with six or so vegetarian dishes, a dollop of steaming rice, *papadoms* (puffed wheat *puri*) and fresh *dahl* (curd). If you're not enormously hungry, try one or two snacks, such as a plate of doughnut-shaped *vadai*, or a pizza-topped *uttapam*. Soothe away the chilies with a *lassi*. You'll soon catch onto the south Indian way of using fingers as expert all-purpose eating utensils – but remember to observe the Indian etiquette of using only your right hand. You'll notice how locals scrupulously clean their hands before settling into their finger meal.

Rail-buffs won't need any encouragement to visit Delhi's interesting **Rail Museum** after lunch, a 15-minute taxi ride away, on Shanti Path tucked behind the Bhutan Embassy in the diplomatic enclave of Chanakyapuri. Within its spacious, tree-filled garden are open-air

Rail Museum

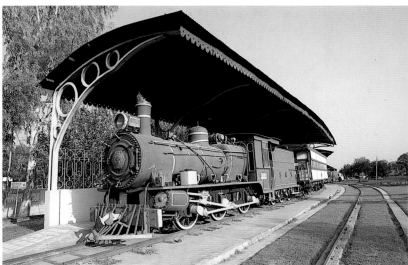

exhibits of antique wooden coaches with period interiors, rusty bogies and rail track fragments. Many coaches were built during the early days of the British Raj and used by maharajahs or viceroys.

Look for the coach built for the Prince of Wales (later Edward VII) when he visited India in 1876. Other highlights include an 1885 steam engine, a 1908 Viceregal dining coach and a museum stuffed with fascinating rail-lore covering the gamut of the colorful history of trains in India. The most eccentric exhibit is the fractured skull of a wild elephant which charged a Calcutta-bound train in 1894. It's possible to pick up original sepia lithographs of antique trains, which from time to time are put on sale. The museum is open everyday except Monday from 9.30 a.m. to 1 p.m., then 1.30 p.m. to 5 p.m.

Lodhi Gardens – walkers' and bird-watchers' paradise

It's probably about 3.30 p.m. now – time to hail a cab for your next stop at **Tibet House** on Lodhi Road, just down the road from Lodhi Gardens. This is a sort of unofficial Tibetan Embassy, run by the Dalai Lama's Trust and representing the affairs of Delhi's some 30,000 Tibetan refugees. Quite often it hums with lecture sessions or debates and visitors are always welcome to sit in. It's an interesting place to visit, with a mini-museum crammed with prized ceremonial objects which the Dalai Lama and his entourage took with them when they fled after the Chinese invasion of Lhasa. Downstairs, a shop sells Tibetan handicrafts and rugs, and the big woollen sweaters and socks make wonderful purchases. It's open from 9 a.m. to 5 p.m., closed on Saturday and Sunday.

As it nears dusk – the Asiatic hour for strolling – you may wish to tackle **Lodhi Gardens** for a peaceful stroll – reached after 15 minutes walk from Tibet House. Here sprawls out a picturesque necropolis of large octagonal tombs from the Sayyid and Lodhi dynasties (1451-1526) set amid leafy parkland, at the center of Delhi's posh residential area and next to the United Nations and Unicef office. The two Afghan dynasties flourished between 1414 and 1526, until Babur defeated the Lodi's at Sikander near Agra and went on to found the Mughal dynasty.

School-boys play cricket on the green and retired civil servants read Hindu epics to rapt cross-legged illiterates under the tamarind trees, *ayahs* (nannies) wander about with toddlers in tow, and MPs and diplomats jog breathlessly, often with their pampered dachshunds, or even with security men lugging rifles. If you've packed your running shoes, this is the place to go.

Tombs are everywhere, some used as gardeners' sheds, often sadly defaced with graffiti. But look especially for the **Bara Gumbad** with its large dome, and adjoining mosque with its well-preserved stucco designs and calligraphy. Opposite is the **Sheesh Gumbad**, which still has much of its blue-tiled roof and exterior inlay floral designs. Also look for **Sikandar Shah Lodhi's tomb** erected in 1450, one of the earliest prototypes of Mughal design.

10. Sunday tour

Lunch at Karims; Car-Parts Bazaar; Jama Masjid's Meena Bazaar; Wrestling Match at Netaji Subhash Park and teeming Sunday Bazaar.

This tour is tailor-made for an adventurous Sunday afternoon in old Delhi, full of wafting spices, crowds and teeming junk bazaars. Start about 2 p.m., take a taxi down to the **Jama Masjid**, where you can either pay off your driver or let him wait for two hours or so.

Seek out **Karim's Restaurant** for a late lunch, plunging into the medieval bustle of this predominantly Muslim enclave south of the mosque. Any one can point the way to Karims, tel: 269880, located in Gali Kababian or the "Alley of Kebabs", just off the cobbled thoroughfare of Motia Mahal. It's just two minutes walk – winding past knots of conversing crochet-capped merchants, loitering buffalos, stalls and shops, tanners and cobblers.

If you're vegetarian, or merely rather fastidious, then Karims will not tickle your taste-buds – with its open-air courtyard kitchen bubbling with mutton, trotters and offal, and sizzling with rows of spiced kebabs laid over charcoal embers. But for almost a century it has earned a cult following in Delhi for its earthy, authentic Muslim food, attracting several thousands of customers a day.

Its most celebrated dish is its breakfast *nahari* (morning lamb curry), and *paya* (lamb's trotters), both simmered to a marrow-rich broth overnight, imbued with *garam masala*, ginger, cloves, fennel and rose petals, and served with *khameeri roti*, a special bread leavened with yoghurt, whole wheat flour and sugar. To sample this, you'll have to make a special trip and be there by 7 a.m. – preferably in the company of an Indian friend to cajole you into your first mouthful, after which you'll become a firm addict – like tens of millions of Indians every morning across north India.

For lunch, try some *shammi* or *seekh kebabs*, before a plate of *firdausi qorma* (lamb curry) and a choice of breads: fluffy *naan*, richly-spiced *kulcha*, paper-thin *roomali roti* or the unusual mint-flavored leavened *sheermal* bread, all fresh from a red-hot iron *tandoor* oven – and quite delicious!

You'll need a stroll after lunch. Walking back towards the Jama Masjid, take a wander through the **Car-parts Bazaar**, which stretches all along the mosque's south side. Even though it's Sunday, this area is still humming with commerce, and for anyone interested in cars, is a wrecker's paradise of smashed cars, with drifting piles of spark plugs, dashboards, speedometers, wing mirrors and head-

Hawking beside the Friday Mosque

lights – and from time to time, rather valuable antique parts lurk unclaimed in the rubble waiting for scrupulous collectors.

On the opposite side of the mosque, you'll find **Meena Bazaar**, a sprawling, incense-scented tangle of ware-crammed stalls. For Chandni Chowk's Muslims, this is the Sunday equivalent of going to the shopping mall.

Aside from occasional pungent whiffs emanating from a nearby chicken market, it's fun to peer at all the accoutrements being sold here: sheaves of rhubarb-colored *burqas*, (the all-encompassing garment worn by Muslim women), lacy caps, fur *fezzes*, Islamic religious cassettes of wailing muezzin cries, reflective silver scripture pictures and plug-in Taj Mahal baubles which shine in the dark. Sinewey chefs skewer kebabs and dole out spoonfuls of *pulao*, a typical Muslim dish of saffron-flavored rice and mutton, onto plates made from leaves.

Retrace your steps through the market to the foot of the steps leading to the Jama Masjid. On your right, you'll see stalls selling rose petals and *attar,* or rose-oil essence, which pilgrims buy to scatter over the shrines of two Muslim martyrs housed inside the red and green building, just opposite.

It should be about 4 p.m. by now, and if you're interested in witnessing something completely different, this is the hour when Delhi's muscle-bound converge on **Netaji Subhash Park** for their **weekly wrestling match**. Getting there involves a walk through the very odiferous poultry and fish markets which line the right side of Meena Bazar – not a pretty sight (or smell!).

As your taxi drove past the park en route to the Jama Masjid this morning, you might have noticed giant lurid cut-out figures of this week's contestants. Stripped to their underpants, and flexing their greased-down muscles, the wrestlers spar in an *akara,* or wrestling pit to cries of applause from the audience. This is a very rough-and-ready form of entertainment – attracting Delhi's auto-rickshaw drivers on their day off – but might appeal to some as a cultural novelty.

Outside the park, along Netaji Subhash Marg's pavement, you'll find an impromptu market set up by Tibetan refugees selling brightly colored woollen knits, and a row of fortune-tellers, tanners, cobblers, quacks, hair-dressers, masseuses and ear-cleaners – surrounded by the little bottles, implements or magic formulas of their trade.

If this part of the tour doesn't appeal to you, then clamber into a taxi and ask to be taken to **Sunday Bazaar**. This is probably Delhi's biggest junk market, stretching for about 2640 feet (800 meters) behind the Red Fort along Mahatma Gandhi Road. It offers every conceivable item, from bird-cages to broken-clocks. There's nothing much to buy really, amongst piles of detritus, unless you have an eye for second-hand odd-ball items, like old-fashioned tools.

Movie-stars among gods and goddesses

11. Ruins and a temple

The ruined city of Feroz Shah Kotla, the National Rose Garden, the Dolls Museum, afternoon tea at the Taj Mahal Hotel, a foray into suburban Delhi to see the Baha'i Temple.

This tour takes you to some of Delhi's lesser-visited sights, for an afternoon of space, peace and contemplative quiet. It's good for any day of the week – but especially Sunday, when shops are closed.

Start your afternoon by driving to the crumbling remains of **Feroz Shah Kotla** on Mahatma Gandhi Road, once the the ancient citadel of Firozabad, Delhi's fifth city. In its heyday, this was a huge, bustling capital, which stretched from North Ridge (near old Delhi) to Hauz Khas, dotted with mosques, reservoirs, colleges, hospitals and hunting lodges. Founded in 1351, it was the creation of Feroz Shah, the third Sultan of the Tughlaq dynasty, whose long 37 year-reign was relatively peaceful, enabling him to indulge his hobby for building and architecture.

Fortress of the third city built by Feroz Shah Tughlaq

Standing on the banks of the **Yamuna River**, the ruins you see here include the **Kushk-i-Feroz**, Feroz Shah's palace and Feroz Shah Kotla, his fortress strong-hold, a once-magnificent complex of palaces, gardens and a mosque. The gardens still blossom, busy with parakeets and squirrels, but the only structure left almost intact is the large **Jami Masjid**, where the ascetic Feroz spent much of his day.

Nearby is one of the two 46-feet (14-meter) high polished sandstone **Ashokan pillars** inscribed with moral edicts from the legendary Buddhist Emperor Ashoka or "Sorrowless One", (273-236 BC) that Feroz Shah transported to Delhi. This one was brought from Topla in Ambala district in Haryana – the other from Meerut in Uttar Pradesh stands on the North Ridge.

Feroz Shah ingeniously floated them both down the Yamuna River encased in ram skin on a buoyant bed of silk cotton and reeds. Thousands of men dragged the pillars into place on a specially-constructed 42-wheel carriage.

Ashoka erected some 30 of these pillars (of which only ten survive) and 18 rock faces across India to spread his faith of *ahimsa,* or non-violence and *dharma*, the Buddhist teachings. When Feroz Shah first came upon these pillars, Ashoka's Brahmi script had still not been deciphered – that remarkable feat was left to British Orientalist

Lotus design of the Bahai Temple

James Prinsep in 1837 – but the Sultan marvelled at them, convinced they possessed magic talismanic value.

From here, stroll down to the **National Rose Garden**, which lie in the southwest corner of Feroz Shah Kotla. By the entrance stands the **Khuni Darwaza** or "Bloody Gate," which apparently served as an entrance to the Afghan king Sher Shah's fortress town of Sher Garh, Delhi's sixth city, whose remains interface those of the Purana Qila, which lies further up Mahatma Gandhi Road. Another monument to look out for near the gardens is **Abdu'n Nabi's Mosque**, built in the 17th century by one of Akbar's devout clerics.

Only doll-addicts or those with children in tow will be interested in the next stop on the itinerary – the **International Dolls Museum**, located on Delhi's "Fleet Street" row of newspaper offices in **Nehru House**, 4, Bahadur Shah Zafar Marg. This involves either a 15-minute walk past carbon dioxide-spewing traffic or a nippy rickshaw ride. It has quite a collection: some 6,000 dolls from 85 different countries. There's an Indian tribal *haute couture* section, and dolls kitted out in the nation's diverse regional costumes. It's open from 10 a.m. to 6 p.m. daily, except on Monday.

It's time to extricate yourself from this noisy, dust-filled part of town and head for the oasis of a hotel coffee shop for afternoon tea. Try the Taj Mahal's **Machan** for some South-Indian coffee and an afternoon snack, or sit out in the sunshine by the hotel's lovely outside pool. Before you leave the hotel, its worth having a browse through their excellent *Khazana* shop, which sells quality leather-ware, jewelry, fabrics, old lithographs and handicrafts. Prices are high, but so is the quality.

It should be about 4.30 p.m. by now, so hail a taxi and make the 20-minute drive out to the modern **Baha'i Temple**, which stands atop Kalkaji Hill, near the suburb of Friend's Colony in south Delhi like a colossal unfolding white marble lotus flower. Delhi Baha'ites are extremely proud of this architectural emblem, which was built from funds donated from Baha'i devotees across the globe, and like to compare it to the Sydney Opera House, and even the Taj Mahal.

It is certainly not the Taj Mahal, although it is made from the same Rajasthani Macrana marble, but it is undeniably impressive. Set in well-tended gardens, each of its sculpted marble "petals" are surrounded by nine pools and walkways, each leading to a different entrance, which apparently denote the many paths leading to God. Inside the prayer hall tapers to 100 feet (30½ meters) high, with no supporting columns, creating a feeling of breathtaking spaciousness and serenity.

The Baha'i faith began in present-day Iran in 1844 by Baha'u'llah, a Persian nobleman, who proclaimed himself the "Promised One", who had been entrusted with a message from God that the path to religious truth lay in the spiritual and social unification of the world. For this he was reviled by all religions and governments, and spent the rest of his life exiled in Constantinople and Adrianople.

In India there are some 1½ million adherents of the faith, and hundreds visit the temple in Delhi each day to worship. Before entering the temple, you'll need to remove your shoes and maintain complete silence, except during the prayer hours at 10 a.m. and 4 p.m. every day. It's most beautiful to visit at sunset, when the temple's polished surface glows oleander-pink and peacocks start their melancholic evening song.

12. On the Gandhi and Nehru trail

Lunch at Claridges Hotel, visits to Gandhi Smitri, Teen Murti House and the riverside ghats.

This is a relaxed afternoon tour, combining visits to historic museum-houses with garden walks. Start with lunch at Claridges Hotel's **Dhaba restaurant**, styled to resemble one of India's numerous roadside *dhabas* or truck stops, with half a real truck – complete with authentic lurid decorations, swastikas and tassels – emerging from its wall. This is the place to sample excellent, earthy north-west frontier and Punjabi fare, especially *tandoor* and bread specialities.

Try the Chicken Kebabs and *Saag Paneer*, a dish of spiced cottage cheese and spinach, accompanied by *tandoori roti* and a *nimbu* soda.

After lunch, it's just a five-minute stroll down Tees January Road to find **Birla House**, now called Gandhi Smitri at No. 5. This was the palatial residence of G.D. Birla, one of India's wealthiest industrialists and a long-time follower and financial supporter of Mahatma Gandhi and Jawaharlal Nehru.

Gandhi came here in September 1947, amid the holocaust of partition after Independence, still weak from a long fast undertaken to protest bloodshed between the Hindus and Muslims in Bengal. At that time Delhi was swollen with refugees, as more than ten million

people migrated in each direction across the newly-divided Punjab – the largest human exodus in history. The price of this operation was literally a holocaust of frenzied communal killing and suffering. While the Indian police seemed powerless to stop the massacres, Gandhi bravely campaigned for tolerance and non-violence. Although Gandhi usually made a point of living ascetically, Birla insisted he stay in the safety of his family home, with its ample flower-filled gardens in which Gandhi conducted his public evening prayer meetings. On 30 January, Gandhi was walking through these gardens when he was assassinated by a Hindu fanatic. All three bullets penetrated his heart. Crying out "He Ram" (O God!), Gandhi collapsed to the ground, dead.

You can walk through the gardens to see where Gandhi died, and inside is a well-documented display of Gandhi's life. For the hundreds who stream through daily, this place has a shrine-like significance. It's open every day from 10 a.m. to 5 p.m., with a filmshow at 3 p.m., a very moving tribute to the magnificence of the man and his ideas.

Hail a taxi or auto-rickshaw to the next historic house on your trail today. On Teen Murti Road, near the diplomatic enclave of Chanakyapuri, stands **Teen Murti House**, the residence of India's first Prime Minister Jawaharlal Nehru from 1948 until his death in 1964. Originally one of colonial New Delhi's star mansions – designed for the British Commander-in-Chief, who was second only to the Viceroy – it appealed to Nehru's Harrow-educated taste. The beautifully kept house and garden now form the Nehru Museum, with furnishings, library, bedroom and desk left as he left them – and the rosebeds still aflower with the blooms Nehru was famous for knotting into his buttonhole each morning. It's open from 10 a.m. to 5 p.m., with filmshows at 11 a.m. and 3 p.m..

Now hail a taxi from the stand just outside and ask to be driven to **Raj Ghat** on the banks of the Yamuna River, reached after a 20-minute drive east along Mahatma Gandhi Road. A simple black marble slab marks the place where Gandhi was cremated a day after his death. The site is surrounded by a cluster of "ideologically-opposed trees" planted by various dignitaries, notably Mikhail Gorbachev, Queen Elizabeth II, Dwight Eisenhower and Ho Chi Min.

You've probably had enough of museums, but it's worth knowing that the **Gandhi Memorial Museum** is just across the road from here. It doesn't have the poignancy of Birla House, but there's a good exhibition and plenty of books to buy.

From Raj Ghat stretches a riverside parkland, pleasant for strolling. Further along is the **Shanti Vana** (Forest of Peace) ghat where members of India's ruling Nehru dynasty were given their funeral pyres, most recently Indira Gandhi in 1984.

Lastly, **Vijay Ghat memorial** is dedicated to Lal Bahadur Shastri, India's second prime minister (died 11 January 1966).

13. Suraj Kund

A drive into Haryana state; the ruins of Suraj Kund; boating on the lake and picnic in the park.

If you have an afternoon to spare, it's well worth making the 10-mile (16-km) drive across the Delhi border into Haryana state to see the enigmatic ampitheater of **Suraj Kund**, the only great ancient Hindu shrine left intact by invading Muslims. It's name literally means "Sun Pool". Dedicated to the Sun God, Surya, it was thought to have been constructed during the 10th century by Raja Suraj Pal, a chieftain of the sun-worshipping Tomar Rajputs.

Set out after lunch, and be prepared for a half-hour's foray through Delhi's dusty suburbs and hamlets before reaching your destination, which lies in the vicinity of Faridabad district. The return taxi fare will come to about Rs200, plus an additional waiting charge. Ordinary taxis aren't able to drive outside the metropolitan limits, but your hotel can easily arrange for a taxi with an All India Tourist Permit that can take you.

The pool of Suraj Kund is surrounded by huge scooped rings of slab-stoned steps, where lizards laze in the afternoon sun. It's pleasant to sit here and contemplate what rituals might have taken place here so many centuries ago. Nearby stands the ruined temple of **Surya**, enmeshed in tussock grass.

Around this ancient relic spans peaceful gardens and a small artificial lake, where row-boats can be rented out. Middle-class Indian families migrate here on Sundays to spread giant hampers out on the grassy slopes to be persistently serenaded by snake-charmers, who unravel their swagbag of cobras at the slightest provocation. It's most peaceful to visit during the weekdays, where you can picnic undisturbed among the ruins, squirrels and peacocks.

If you need a place to break for afternoon tea (or to use restrooms), try the **Raj Hans Hotel** nearby.

It's especially worth making this trip if you are in Delhi during the **first week of February** when the colorful **Crafts Mela** is held, attracting craftsmen and artisans all over India, who come to demonstrate their skills and sell their wares. There is a carnival atmosphere with puppet shows, camel and elephant rides, dare-devil acrobats, folk dances and songs.

Weavers at a crafts fair

Nightlife

Although Delhi never claimed to be one of the world's cosmopolitan cities, you may be surprised to find that discos, parties and an array of cultural events exist to keep you amused until the wee hours.

By and large, Delhi's socializing revolves around its marble mausoleum-style five-star hotels, where restaurants and bars are air-conditioned and serve imported wines and spirits.

Discos have a cult following among Delhi's upwardly mobile, and on Friday and Saturday nights are packed to the rafters, generally opening around 9 p.m. and shutting up around three or four in the morning. Cover charges are usually about Rs200-250, and bar prices are reasonable if you stick to Indian beer. Peculiar **dress codes** in force in Delhi bar entry to men in jeans, slip-ons or running shoes, but okays nylon safari-suits, gold medallions and snakeskin shoes.

The best of the bunch is the **Ghungroo** at the Maurya Sheraton, a dark, flashing pit full of be-bopping turbanned Sikhs, African students and other night lizards dancing to the latest pop music. Sometimes there are impromptu dancing competitions that bring all of Delhi's Prince-lookalikes to the floor.

The Taj Mansingh's **Number One** has a regular following among

The thrill of the film industry

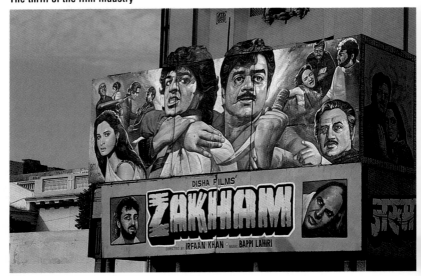

Delhi's Maruti-driving moneyed young. The Hyatt Regency has **Oasis**, a flashy basement disco best visited on its busy "Ladies Night" every Wednesday. Other late-night alternatives include the Holiday Inn's **Annabelle's**, and the Taj Palace's **My Kind of Place**, a haven of Bangalore rococo decor where sedate over-30s go for whisky sodas and nostalgic 1950s classics not on the lively disco scale.

Cabarets: those with an eccentric taste in the sleazy or simply idle curiosity will appreciate the spectacle of a Delhi cabaret, which offers, pardon the pun, a peek beneath the city's skirts. Delhi has several, most of them facing almost constant threat of closure, enhancing their speak-easy atmosphere. The most reliably open is in the **Rajdoot Hotel** (tel: 699583) at 14 Mathura Road; every taxi driver unerringly knows where it is. Inexplicably, it has become an unofficial tourist attraction for crowds of visiting Soviet technocrats and tourists, who nurse ice-cream sodas while watching the stage antics of a tinsel-bikini clad, black-lipsticked nymph-no-longer. Friday and Saturday night shows are advertised in the *Hindustan Times*.

Aside from hotel bars and nightclubs, it helps to have some local contacts. Visitors drawn into well-connected party circles are taken behind the city's "Brocade Curtain" on a whirl of socials in homes and exclusive clubs. Here, dress, manners and informed conversation are everything. Tradition ensures that while guests are plied with drinks, food often doesn't arrive till past midnight. By the time it does, your surroundings may have become an amiable blur of perfume, silk saris, handle-bar moustaches and tinkling laughs. Guests tend to eat quickly, then immediately melt away into the night. Not surprisingly, whisky on an empty stomach followed by rich spicy food can prove taxing on the physique. The best counter-measure is to have a snack before going out, and then drink and eat lightly.

If you don't have Delhi contacts to savor the local scene, and even if you do, sample something of India's cultural heritage. The country's top classical dancers and musicians perform here regularly. Scan the morning's *Times of India* or *Indian Express* for daily listings of what's on, the *Delhi Diary* sold at most newsstands, or consult the Tourist Office's fortnightly *Program of Events*. Performances tend to start around 6.30 p.m. There is a **central ticket office** at the Cottage Industries Emporium on Janpath. Popular venues for performances are in the What To Know section at the back of this book.

One regular event to catch is the **Dances of India** program at the Parsi Anjuman Hall, (tel: 275978/3317831), at Bahadur Shah Zafar Marg, Delhi Gate; a popular showcase of folk, classical and tribal dances starts nightly at 7 p.m. Otherwise, both the **Taj Mahal** and the **Taj Palace hotels** have dinner-dance and music performances beginning at 9 p.m. at their Indian restaurants.

Hindi Movies: if you want to experience their technicolor thrills, wet saris and outrageous fortunes, join flare-trousered youths at the **Regal Cinema** in Connaught Place or the modern **Sheila Cinema** opposite New Delhi Railway Station.

Day TRips

Agra and Fatehpur Sikri

Full day

Many people visit Delhi merely to reach Agra, the medieval city of the famous Taj Mahal, 126 miles (204 km) southeast, just two hours by train. Yet a few linger long in Agra, which despite its magnificent Mughal Red Fort, mausoleums and handicrafts, also has the reputation of a tourist trap swamped with assertive touts. Ideally, make Agra your base for the rewarding trip out to the deserted city of Fatehpur Sikri. If you want to stretch the day trips into two or three days, plan to stay at least one night at the nearby Bharatpur, site of India's largest and gloriously scenic bird sanctuary.

Agra

It's most convenient to take the speedy **2002 Shatabdi Express,** which leaves New Delhi Railway Station at 6.30 a.m. and arrives at 8.45 p.m. Tickets can be purchased in advance through a travel agent, or from the tourist office on the 2nd floor of the New Delhi railway Station. Present your passport and pay in hard currency or traveler's checks. It's open from 9 a.m. to 5 p.m. and breaks for lunch between 1 p.m. and 1.30 p.m. and is closed on Sunday.

By Indian standards the Shatabdi Express is unusually luxurious with all its cabins air-conditioned and the added bonus of being served surprisingly good free meals by a cumberbund-wearing waiter.

Once you arrive at **Agra station** you can arrange your transport for the day and if necessary, purchase your return transport for the day too. Head straight for the **Government of India stand** at the station which offers reliable drivers and a fixed rate of Rs350 for a day's taxi hire. If you end up having to take pot luck with Agra's inevitable stream of strident touts, make sure your driver agrees to a similar fee for the day and to drop you back at the station by 7.30 p.m., in time to catch the 8.10 p.m. Shatabdi Express back to Delhi.

Make the Taj Mahal your first stop. India's most visited tourist attraction is still the most enduring symbol of love. With its milky mirage-like beauty, this 17th-century architectural masterpiece never fails to penetrate even the hearts of hardened travelers. The elaborate

80

mausoleum was built by Mughal Emperor Shah Jahan as a tribute to his beloved Empress Mumtaz Mahal, his 'Light of the Palace' who, after 17 years of blissful if strenuous marriage, died at the age of 39 while delivering her 14th child. "Empire has no sweetness, life itself has no relish for me now," Shah Jehan mourned at the news of her death. For the next 35 years of his life he devoted himself to his only other reigning passion — architecture.

The Taj Mahal was completed in 1659 after 21 years of construction by some 20,000 laborers, including artisans from Italy and special consultants who went on to design Shah Jahan's fabled **Peacock Throne**. Beneath its tons of seamless white Macrana marble lies plain red sandstone fashioned to jewel-like brilliance by exquisite *pieta dura* inlay of precious stones and Urdu verses from the Koran, fretted marble screens and bulbous domes.

Classical Mughal symmetry is achieved by precisely laid-out gardens and water pavilions and by balancing the great tomb with four towering minarets and two subsidiary buildings, a mosque and an assembly hall. Silhouetted against the sky, it gives the illusion of floating above the reflected image in the central waterhouse.

The entrance level contains false tombs of Mumtaz and Shah Jahan whose bodies were laid to rest about 20 ft (6 meters) underground in a lower burial vault. Both sets of tombs are inlaid with hundreds of jasper, emeralds, sapphires and other precious stones but Mumtaz's sarcophagi are more profusely engraved with floral patterns in accordance with Shah Jahan's wish that his wife's grave be continually strewn with flowers.

Next, see the red sandstone Agra Fort across the bend in the Yumana River. Built by the Mughal Emperor, Akhbar the Great between 1566 and 1573, this impregnable citadel is encircled by crenellated battlements, wide moats, massive watch-towers and giant gateways. The well-preserved interior of palaces, pavilions and gardens give a real sense of the fort's past grandeur, and is far more impressive than the much-plundered Red Fort in Delhi. Aside from Akbar's austere, earth-bound former living quarters, few of its original buildings remain, for his son Jahangir and grandson Shah Jahan replaced them with more opulent structures. Most of the fort's

The splendor of the Taj Mahal

interior belongs to Shah Jahan, who created an ornate labyrinth of lavish marble palaces and pavilioned gardens, notably his 40-pillared **Diwan-i-am** (public audience hall), the **Diwan-i-Khas** (private audience hall), once extravagantly dripping with gold, sliver and precious stones and the exquisite **Moti Masjid** (Pearl Mosque). Look for a **giant ring** outside the Diwan-i-Am which used to act as a leg-bracelet for the elephants who trampled unfortunate criminals to death. Also look for the **Khas Mahal**, Shah Jahan's private apartment, the **Sheesh Mahal** (Mirror Palace) and the octogonal **Musamman Burj**, Jasmine Tower, named for its adornment of flower-wreathed columns. Here, Shah Jahan spent the last of his life as a prisoner of his fanatical son, Aurangzeb. From here, the deposed monarch could gaze across the river to his finest creation, the Taj Mahal.

Make your next taxi stop to **Itmad-ud-Daulah's tomb** a 15-minute drive on the opposite bank of the Yamuna River, about 9½ miles (15 km) northeast. Nicknamed the baby Taj, it is less frequented, smaller, yet somehow more delicately beautiful than its famous, grander cousin. Completed in 1628, it is the final resting place of Mirza Ghiyas Beg (alias Itmud-ud-Daulah, or "Pillar of the State"). It was commissioned by his powerful wife, and was the first Mughal tomb to incorporate the Persian technique of *pieta dura*, the inlay of semi-precious stones in marble; a feminine touch prevails in its intricate geometric and floral motifs.

By now you'll feel like lunch. The best place for stylish, authentic Mughlai cuisine is the Mughal Sheraton's **Nauratna restaurant** excellent for succulent, spiced *tandoori kebabs*, *rogan josh* (curried lamb), mutton *biryani* and rich *rasgulla* (cream cheese balls in sugared rose water). There are also lunch-time *thali* platters with spiced dishes, Indian breads and chutneys.

After lunch, about 2 p.m., set off for **Fatehpur Sikri**, which lies  23 miles (37 km) west of Agra, about an hour's drive. You won't regret the detour. To walk this elaborate metropolis, filled with rust-colored sandstone and marble palaces, pleasure domes, gardens, bath-houses and stables, is to visualize with almost uncanny detail, the refined decadence of the 400 year-old Mughal court. It was the Mughal empire's most fleeting

Fatehpur Sikri

capital – inhabited for only 14 years – and arguably its most magnificent; still almost perfectly preserved.

As the story goes, the mightiest of the Mughals, Akbar, was inspired to build Fatehpur Sikri, or "City of Victory", in gratitude to a local Sufi Muslim holy man, Sheikh Salim Chisthi, who successfully prophesied the birth of the emperor's three male heirs. Construction of Fatehpur Sikri and its encircling 9-mile (14-km) boundary walls took a decade, commencing in 1565. Yet by 1586, Akbar was forced to abandon his city, apparently when the water supply dried up, prompting a mass migration back to Agra.

There are two entrances to the city. To the left is the monumental 177-ft (54-meters) high **Buland Darwaza**, Victory Gate, built to commemorate Akbar's invasion of Gujarat in 1573. Majestic steps lead into its courtyard, beyond which shelters an impressive **Jama Masjid**, or Friday Mosque, said to be a copy of the main mosque at Mecca, and the white marble jewel-like tomb of Salim Sheikh Chisthi, adorned with latticed *jali* screens and serpentine tendrils. It was begun by Akbar after the holy man's death in 1571, but finished by Shah Jahan, who added much of its exquisite *pieta dura* work. Childless women come to pray here, and tie colored threads to the screens to make a wish.

Akbar's elegant palace citadel lies through the Shahi Darwza gate. First are the extensive *zenana* or harem quarters, over which Akbar's powerful Rajput wife, Jodh Bai, presided from her *purdah*-screened salon. Two favorite wives had separate houses: Akbar's Christian wife from Goa, Maryam, lived in the so-called Golden Palace, and his Turkish wife, Sultana Begum, had a marble pavilion, once studded with semi-precious stones. Eunuches used to guard the *zenana*'s many interior gates, preventing jealous wives and concubines from learning of Akbar's nightly wanderings.

Look especially for the five-storied **Panch Mahal** where Akbar loved to linger with his harem and books on summer evenings and the **Diwan-i-Khas**, dominated by this massive central **Lotus Throne Pillar** embellished with an eclectic *potpurri* of religious symbols. Closeby is the **Diwan-i Am** and its upstairs *Khwabagh*, (house of dreams), Akbar's private bedroom, the Astrologer's Seat, the Treasury and the Paschesi Courtyard, where Akbar ordered gauzily-clad slave girls to move a giant chessboard as pieces in *paschesi*, a game similar to ludo. You may need a **map** and wish to hire a **licensed guide** – both are available at the **Shahi Darwaza**.

From Fatehpur Sikri, **Bharatpur's Keoladeo National Park** lies 10½ miles (17 km) away, if you wish to extend your stay. An ornithologist's paradise, it is one of the world's finest bird sanctuaries with over 10.4 sq miles (29 sq km) of freshwater marshland, originally developed by the Maharajah of Bharatpur for his legendary duck shoots. It's best to stay overnight so you can witness the miracle of sunrise which rouses all the exotic birdlife to swoop and plunge against the dawn sky. In Bharatpur, which is just minutes away from the sanctuary, try old-world charm at the delightful **Golbargh Palace Hotel**, once a royal guest house, tel: 3349, or the more functional **Saras Tourist Bungalow**, tel: 37003, both moderately priced. The nicest in-park option is the **Shanti Kutir Forest Rest House**, the renovated former royal hunting lodge, which must be booked in writing.

Dining Experience

India is home to one of the world's most varied and extraordinary cuisine, with a myriad of regional flavors, textures and preparation styles to tantalize the taste buds.

As the nation's capital, Delhi offers some great eating experiences. After a few meals and a foray to the city's varied eateries, you'll realize than Indian food is infinitely more than merely "curry".

You can gourmandize to your heart's content on the city's own historic cuisines which traces its lineage from the courtly kitchens of the Mughal Emperors and is named after them as Mughlai. You can sample a little of everything from India, and savor India's regional diversity with each mouthful. Add to this the raft of luxury hotels with restaurants specializing in foreign cuisines such as French, Italian, Chinese and Japanese, and you'll never run out of good things to eat.

Generally Delhi's best food is served in its hotel restaurants, as enthusiastically patronized by well-heeled locals as visiting tourists – and a vital part of Delhi's fashionable so-called "five-star culture". You may have to reserve beforehand. Other than these, you can choose from a growing array of established restaurants and eating houses scattered across town. Here are some best daytime bets:

Breakfast

Hyatt Regency Hotel. The coffee shop has an enormous buffet with continental and delicious south Indian breakfast specialities, with fresh fruit juices and in-house pastries from 6 a.m. to 10 a.m.

Karims, Jama Masjid, Old Delhi. Truly adventurous eaters will enjoy sampling the early-morning Muslim breakfast staples of *nihari* (morning lamb curry) and *khameer roti*, followed by a brisk stroll

watching Chandni Chowk's residents in the throes of waking up. Be there by 6.30 to 7 a.m.

Lunch

La Rochelle, Oberoi Intercontinental Hotel. For a quiet oasis of classy chic this is the place. Very elegant, with French cuisine. You can dine on quails, oysters, steaks and imported wines at rather extravagant prices, or opt for the very reasonably-priced lunch-time buffet, which runs from noon until 2.30 p.m.

Maurya Sheraton Hotel. Delhi's south Indian community flocks to the coffee shop's excellent buffet of freshly-cooked regional specialities such as *dosas, idlis, uttapams* and *thali* lunches cooked by resident chefs. Only on Saturday and Sunday from 11.30 a.m. to 3 p.m.

Afternoon tea

The Lawn, Imperial Hotel. Very colonial, relaxing garden haven for tea and sandwiches under a beach umbrella. Gaylords, (tel: 311-715), B 16 Regal Building, Connaught Place.
Another quirky Raj-era retreat, with plush chairs, chandeliers and

cumberbund-clad waiters. It's a good place for a break in shopping to enjoy South Indian coffee and samosas.

Emperor's Lounge, Taj Mahal Hotel. Delhi's only equivalent of "Breakfast at Tiffany's". After 4 p.m., enjoy soothing classical music by a talented quartet, tea and cakes.

Evening cocktails

Again, hotels have a monopoly. The rooftop **Skylark Bar**, Oberoi Intercontinental, is particularly stylish and sometimes has live jazz. Other subdued, elegant options include the Hyatt Regency Hotel's **Piano Bar**, the Maurya Sheraton Hotel's **Madira**, and the Taj Mahal hotel's **Captain's Cabin**, which has the best *hors d'oeuvres*. The Imperial Hotel's quaint old-world **Garden Bar** has charm. Bar prices can be steep if you order imported wine or spirits.

Non-alcoholic sundowners can be very pleasant at the leafy outdoor cafe **Aashiana**, which is nestled in Lodhi Gardens just off the main Lodhi Road.

A taste of India

Delhi is probably the best place in the world to sample delicious authentic Mughlai and North Indian food.

Mughlai dishes are strongly meat-based and very rich, with sauces redolent of thick yoghurt, fried onions, saffron and nuts brought by the Mughals from Persia in the 16th century. *Rogon josh*, (curried lamb), *gushtaba* (spicy meat pounded to *pate*-consistency, formed into balls and simmered in spiced yoghurt) and *biryani* (mutton or lamb in orange-colored rice, sprinkled with rose water, almonds and dried fruits) are some well known Mughlai dishes. Other meat specialities include the popular *shami* and *seekh kebabs* cooked over a charcoal grill on skewers.

Vegetable dishes include *dal makhnai*, a rich, spiced dish of lentils with coriander and cream, *shahi paneer,* cheese in cream and tomatoes, *khatte aloo,* spiced potato or *baingan mumtaz*, stuffed eggplant. These are served with a variety of breads, such as doughy *naans*, fried *paratha*, stuffed *kulcha*, and paper-thin *roomali roti*. In addition there is the famous Mughlai *nav-ratan* (nine gems) chutney and pickles.

From the North-West Frontier Province (now in Pakistan) comes the famous legacy of *tandoori* (clay oven) baked chicken, lamb and fish dishes. These dishes attain their distinctive succulence from being marinated in a mixture of yoghurt, crushed garlic, spices and sometimes papaya pulp, and then skewered over the *tandoor* oven's glowing coals. Don't be alarmed by the fiery red of your *tandoori* chicken – the color comes from the marinade, not from being lathered in tongue-singeing chillies!

Earthy Punjabi favorites include spiced *saag*, made from spinach-like mustard leaves and cornflour bread or *makai ki roti*, and the calorie-laden *gajar ka halwa*, or carrot pudding.

Longevity-conscious south Indians traditionally serve an array of light, but fiercely hot curries on as a *thali*, with steaming rice, chutneys, pickles and *puris* – either on a well-washed banana leaf or on a *thali*, a large round metal tray filled with little bowls that are constantly refilled. Other specialities include the breakfast staples – the popular *dosa*, a form of *crepe* made from lightly fermented rice flour and stuffed with spiced potato, and steamed rice-cake *idlis*, both eaten with fresh coconut chutney and *sambhar*, a chilli-laced lentil soup. Finish your meal with a cup of steaming Mysore coffee served in a metal tumbler.

Desserts are mainly very sweet milk/curd-based puddings and confections like mouth-watering *kulfi* ice-cream, flavored with cardamon, pistachio nuts and saffron, *rasgullas*, (cream cheese balls in rose syrup), and *burfi halwa* sweets, covered in wafer-thin silver paper. *Gulab Jamun*, (spongy ground-almond balls), and *jalebi*, (cartwheel-shaped sweets) both come dripping with honeyed syrup.

Some Indian meals end with a betel leaf *paan*, which, so it is claimed, cleanses the palate and aids digestion. Restaurants serve them on the house, and there are *paan wallahs* on the street, who use *paan* leaves as a base on which to dab lime, *catechu* paste, scented tobacco, sliced coconut and other tidbits all of which you chew, swallow the juices and spit out when you've had enough.

The fabled furnace-like heat of Indian food, particularly South Indian food – causing the unwary eater to turn bright red and blink back tears – can be an occupational hazard of experimentation, better soothed by *raita* (yoghurt side-dish) or a gulp of a yoghurt *lassi* than water.

Mughlai and North Indian food

Dum Pukht, Maurya Sheraton Hotel. One of India's most outstanding restaurants, offers sumptuous aristocratic 16th-century cuisine from Lucknow. Stylish and gilt-edged, with dishes served on silver plates.

Preparing sweetmeats

Service is impeccable. Whatever else you order make sure you start with *kakori kebab* – rounds of spiced lamb dish pounded to such delicacy that it literally melts in the mouth; first created for a toothless old Nawab and served with mint chutney. Reservations are required.

Kandahar, The Oberoi. Excellent Mughlai and North-West Frontier fare in classy European surrounds, subdued lighting and elegant silverware. True to Mughlai form you'll find no knives or forks on the table.

Bukahara, Maurya Sheraton Hotel. Renowned for its delicious Frontier food, notably its succulent *raan*, chicken *tikka* and charcoal-grilled *kebab*s in mock-rustic surroundings. Guests are invited to slip on aprons, eat with their fingers and sip frothy Indian beer from pewter goblets and watch chefs at work behind huge glass windows. This place is so popular, they don't take bookings after 8.30 p.m.

Haveli, Taj Mahal Hotel. Classic, hearty Mughlai, Peshwari and Hyderabadi dishes served amid tasteful surroundings, where you'll also be entertained by an evening performance of traditional dance and music.

Handi, Taj Palace Intercontinental Hotel. Regional north and west Indian cuisine, with an evening performance of *ghazals* (songs) and dance.

Frontier, Ashoka Hotel. Authentic North-West Frontier and Punjabi specialities in convivial surroundings, but with strumming minstrels who doggedly serenade your table – something you either adore or suffer.

Open-air dining

Corbetts, Clandges Hotel. Tandoor and barbeque specialities. Delightful setting in pseudo-jungle, echoing with recorded animal and forest sounds.

Moti Mahal, (tel: 273-011), Daryaganj, off Netaji Subhash Marg. An outdoor restaurant with good Mughlai food and a fairly rough-and-ready atmosphere, best when locals arrive to *encore* the evening dancers and *ghazal* singers.

Less Salubrious Locations

Tandoor, Hotel President, (tel: 277-836), Asaf Ali Road. Excellent North-Indian food, especially *kebab* specialities. Musicians perform classical *sitar* music after 9 p.m.

Karims, Jama Masjid. (tel: 269-880) Earthy locale in the middle of old Delhi; very authentic Islamic atmosphere. Try *shammi* or *seekh kebabs*, *firdausi qorma* (lamb curry) and hearty *naan* bread. As with any eatery in old Delhi after 9 p.m., you'll observe rows of urchins patiently congregating outside – after the last diner has left they'll be given the night's scraps!

The **Nizamuddin branch** of Karims is more souped-up, but tends to use extra-liberal quantities of *ghee* (clarified butter).

Kwality, (tel: 350-110), 7 Regal Building, Connaught Place. Of its large menu, Mughlai dishes are best. Good for lunch-time splurge.

South Indian vegetarian

Dasaprakash, Hotel Ambassador, (tel: 694-966). Located in a cavernous, lamp-lit dome and always filled with avidly-eating guests. Their three-course *thali* meal is classic south Indian, excellent and enormously filling. House specialities are fresh grape juice, *lassis* and creamy mango milk shakes.

Woodlands, Lodhi Hotel (tel: 362-422). Recommended for satisfying dinner-time *thali* meals. Open all day for south Indian snacks.

Sagar, (tel: 617-832), 18 Defense Colony Market. Very authentic, freshly-prepared south Indian food, well-worth the detour into suburban Delhi.

Sona Rupa, (tel: 586-509) 46 Janpath. All-day south Indian fast-food, with freshly-prepared *dosas*, *idlis*, *dahi vadas* and *uttapams*. The downstairs section is very basic and extremely cheap, popular with office workers. Upstairs is a lunch and dinner-time buffet.

Coconut Grove, Ashok Yatri Niwas Hotel. Good vegetarian lunch and dinner *thali* meals, as well as non-vegetarian and Bengali dishes.

Others

Goanese

Captain Cabin, Taj Mahal Hotel. Also doubles as a bar with good *flambeau* specialities and grilled steaks, but the Goan chef makes his presence felt. Try the Prawns *Vindaloo*, a whopping platter of spicy king prawns on steaming bed of rice.

Seafood

Fisherman's Wharf, (tel:698123) A-1 Moolchand Shopping Complex, Defence Colony. If you yearn for seafood in land-locked Delhi, this is the place to come. It's probably the best place to satisfy cravings for fresh fish, king prawns, mussels and lobster. Standards of hygiene are high – you can never be too fussy about seafood, especially in Delhi. Try their delicious *tandoori* pomfret, sold at seasonal cost price.

Chinese

It's possible to dine well on Chinese food in Delhi – virtually all the main hotels have Chinese chefs, some of them from Calcutta, where most of India's Chinese community live, and others from Hong Kong and Singapore. The best restaurants import their ingredients, and what they serve, mostly Cantonese and some Szechuan dishes, is comparable with the finest Chinese food anywhere in the world.

Taipan, The Oberoi. Rated very highly by resident Chinese diplomats. Elegant decor. Szechuan food.

Tea House Of The August Moon, Taj Palace Intercontinental Hotel. Szechuan, Cantonese and dim-sum dishes. Eye-catching decor styled after a pagoda garden.

Pearls, Hyatt Regency Hotel. Szechuan food.

House Of Ming, Taj Mahal Hotel. Excellent authentic Szechuan and Cantonese food.

Golden Phoenix, Le Meridien. Cantonese and Szechuan.

Fujiya, 12/14 Malcha Marg. Extremely popular for its "Indianized" Chinese food.

Japanese

Tokyo, Hotel Ashoka. Largely successful, experimental bid to woo Delhi's large Japanese community. The chicken *yakatori* is delicious, but be wary of eating raw fish so far from the sea.

French

The Orient Express, Taj Palace Intercontinental Hotel. Delhi's best French restaurant. Also offers Spanish and Italian dishes, with an extensive imported wine list. Decor simulates the dining car of the vintage Paris-Istanbul train.

La Rochelle, The Oberoi.

Le Pierre, Meridien Hotel.

Italian

Valentinos, Hyatt Regency. Ultra-smart decor with an Italian chef in the kitchen responsible for excellent *pasta* creations, *zabaglione* and home-made ice-cream.

Casa Medici, Taj Mahal Hotel.

American Fast Food

Nirula's, L-Block Connaught Place. Pseudo-American fast food parlor, complete with french fries, "buffalo" burgers, thick-shakes and pizzas. This is the "in" place with Delhi's young jean-clad students and hungry tourists. The complex also includes Delhi's oldest Chinese restaurant, a cake shop, an ice-cream parlor and two popular stand-up fast food annexes.

Wimpy Bar, 15 Janpath. The subcontinent's only Wimpy Bar – a cultural novelty. It serves burgers made from everything except beef; fries and "Campa Cola."

Vegetables – fresh from the village

Shopping

If you plan to return home laden with exotic purchases, you'll find Delhi's shops and bazaars overflowing with remarkable treasures at very affordable prices. Although Delhi produces only a fraction of India's arts and crafts, it is the country's premier showcase for the best top-quality handicrafts, textiles and wares. But you'll also have to comb through plenty of mass-produced junk and an army of wily traders, so it pays to be eclectic in your selection, and search around before giving way to unabashed impulse buying.

Before you set out on a shopping spree, here are some helpful tips to help you on your way.

It's best to start with browsing through the fixed-price government-run emporia, where you'll gain an insight into the range, quality and price of goods to expect in the smaller shops, stalls and bazaars elsewhere. When buying pricier items, especially carpets or jewelry, make sure you receive a detailed receipt, as you may need to declare your purchases when you arrive home. Avoid being taken to any shop by a tout, rickshaw or taxi driver, or even the helpful local guide you may have employed – since unbeknown to you, the price you pay for any item immediately escalates as the shop-owner is obliged to pay them a sizable commission.

Formal shopping hours are from 10 a.m. to 5 p.m., Monday to Saturday. Government offices are supposedly open during lunch, but are in a state of *siesta*. Almost nothing opens on Sunday. **Weekly markets** include **Meena Bazaar** behind the Jama Masjid (Sunday), **Sunday Bazaar** held below the walls of the Red Fort, and the religious-orientated bazaar by Hanuman's Temple on **Baba Kharak Singh Marg** (Tuesday).

Bargaining etiquette. Outside the emporia and hotel arcades, bargaining is nothing less than a way of life. Traders expect their customers to haggle, and are inwardly astonished if items are purchased without even a hint of dissent.

Certainly, once you have experienced the satisfaction of whittling down the price of a carpet, silver necklace or carved statue, you'll be

92

hooked. Use your acting ability – traders do their showmanship routine, offering syrupy tea, and pulling out stock so that their shop takes on the appearance of a sty-pen – and you should do your part by appearing uninterested in the items you most covet, by picking out little defects, and disdainfully scorning the prices being quoted. The last stage of bargaining involves getting up, shaking your head and commenting on how the price is just too high. Usually you won't get far before having your shirt sleeves tugged back inside, with prices dropping with each shrug of your shoulders. Bear in mind that no merchant is going to sell at anything less than his cost price – and they'll often try to sell goods at up to 70 percent higher than that.

But of course bargaining is only the means to the end. When you see something that you really want, or that you know will make a perfect gift for someone, don't feel that if you can't whittle the price down then it's not worth having. In India, as anywhere, quality and fine workmanship will always come with a price-tag attached.

The Government Emporia

The **Central Cottage Industries Emporium** on Janpath is the best-stocked and most central. This two-storied all-India crafts department store has everything from Rajasthani slippers and Orissan wall hangings to South Indian temple lamps to Kashmiri walnut-wood carvings. Upstairs there's a huge variety of brilliant Indian textiles, silks and *saris*, a must for those planning to have clothes tailored either in Delhi or when they arrive home. Items can be gift-wrapped, packed and shipped with minimal hassle. An efficient booking counter is located downstairs which sells tickets for Delhi's cultural performances, and outside is a cafe, bookshop and an office of the Archaeological Survey.

On the other side of Connaught Place on **Baba Kharak Singh Marg** you'll find the row of **individual state emporiums**, which make for fascinating browsing.

Roadside glass-bangle seller

What to buy where

Fabrics and embroidery

India has a rich and glorious tradition of hand-crafted textiles, with a dizzying array of regional techniques, patterns, prints and embroidery styles. The subject requires a thick book by itself.

To get an idea of the tremendous variety, make a special trip to the **Cottage Industries Emporium's first floor** section. Exquisite gold-threaded silk from Karnataka, Kashmiri paisley wool, Rajasthani mirror-work and tie-dyed or *bhandej* fabrics, Madras cotton, Orissa's double *ikat* weaves, Gujarati intricately-meshed *patola*, Mughal-influenced *Varanasi* brocade are just some of the regional fabrics you can see here. There is silk of every color and quality, including the nubbed or shot silk, and prices start at about Rs100 a meter, going much higher. Downstairs you'll find the unusual and decorative Kashmiri *crewel* work furnishing fabric.

On Baba Kharak Singh Marg, go to Ambapali (Bihar) emporium for fine raw silk, Gujari (Gujarat) for embroidered, mirror-studded fabric for wall-hangings, and patola saris and Cauvery (Karnataka) for frothy Bangalore silk chiffon and crepe.

For **exquisite brocades** go to **Benaras House**, N-13 Connaught Place, opposite Scindia House. **Traditional handloom fabrics**, such as *khadi* – the rough, rustic-looking hand-spun and hand-woven cloth popularized by Mahatma Gandhi – can be found at **Handloom House** at 9 A Connaught Place and the better-stocked **Khadi Gramodyog Bhavan** at 24 Regal Building, Connaught Place.

Ornate, tinsel-fringed Hindu **wedding saris, silks and embroidered fabrics** are fun to seek out in **Kinari Gulli** (near Chandhi Chowk), along with plumed brocade turbans, *papier mâché* masks, necklaces of rupees and outrageous head-gear for fancy-dress parties.

Antiques and neo-antiques

Bear in mind that it's **illegal to export anything over 100 years old**, so that it's better to go for "antique" replicas of more recent, vintage, which is just as pleasing to the eye.

For neo-antiques and curios you need go no further than **Sunder Nagar Market**, located mid-way between the Oberoi Hotel and Purana Qila, with some 25 shops. You'll find prices are expensive, so take always take plenty of time to browse before buying. At Sundar Nagar, you'll find a large range of high quality old paintings, ivory, real and imitation Mughal miniatures, painted wooden dowry boxes, jewelry, bronzes, wooden statues, antique textiles and heavy ornate Indian furniture from all over India.

Other places to search out include the **Red Fort arcade, Chawri Bazaar**, the **Mehra Brothers shops** at E 328 Street 4 and **M Block Market**, both in Greater Kailash II.

Rugs and carpets

Indian carpets are highly coveted – especially the exceptionably fine hand-made Kashmiri carpets, usually woven in Persian designs in various combinations of silk and wool. Throughout India, carpets are usually produced over a period of six months to four years on large wooden looms by teams of very young boys whose plight is not one that Amnesty International would approve of. Because Indian carpets are so popular, Delhi's markets are flooded with inferior mass-produced ones – particularly those made with cotton-derivative "staple" yarn which imitates the appearance of silk but looks "cheap" and is less durable.

Unless you have a professional knowledge of the trade, you should always be very careful when buying a carpet – but take heart, because prices can become extremely tempting after a bout of bargaining.

Here are some tips: **Check the content and knot** of the carpet regardless of what the salesman tells you. A silk carpet will weigh at

least 2 kilograms (4½ lb) less than yarn staple or wool. But the true test is to pluck out a knot and burn it — staple yarn ignites easily, but pure silk smoulders slowly. Of course few carpet dealers are going to be very happy about this!

Another test is to check the number of knots per square inch on the reverse of the carpet. A good silk or wool carpet should have about 360 knots per square inch, but the finest carpets have as many as 700.

Far less expensive are *dhurries*, the decorative hand-woven woolen or cotton rugs made mostly in north India. Most *dhurries* are made of silk (natural silk being more expensive than synthetic silk) cotton, wool or a combination of these materials. They come in all sizes and designs, but most are made in fashionable pastel colors, with floral, star and geometrical motifs. One shop worth trying out is **Yak International**, 44 Ring Road, Lajpat Nagar. They also have a shop in Hotel Kanishka along Ashoka Road, but you'll find better prices at the large Ring Road showroom.

Also popular are the Kashmiri *namadas*, brightly chain-stitched rugs made from pounded fleece, or crewel-work floor coverings which have an underside of white cotton fabric.

You can find **Tibetan carpets**, with their motifs of dragons and snow lions, at **Tibet House**, Lodhi Road and at the **Tibetan Self-Help Handicrafts**, 23 Masjid Road, Jangpura, located in the Tibetan refugee camp in north Delhi.

Make sure you scrutinize the carpet for any design or color faults, and ask to be given a certificate of origin to save possible customs duty or VAT payments when you get home.

At the **Cottage Industries Emporium**, the **Kashmir Emporium**, and the **Kashmir Govt Arts Emporium** at 25 B Connaught Place, you can generally be sure of what you are buying, and can trust them to ship your carpet safely home.

Soft furnishings and tableware.

For traditional hand-block fabrics, pretty quilts, European-style garments and fashionable tableware, three shops stand out as exceptional. They are **The Shop**, Regal Building in Connaught Place, and **Anokhi** located in a shopping complex just opposite the Ashoka Hotel. It's worth making a special detour out into the suburbs to track down **Fab India** at 14, N-Block in Greater Kailash I, to peruse their beautiful and impressive range of Western-style curtain and furnishing fabrics.

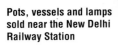

Pots, vessels and lamps sold near the New Delhi Railway Station

Some miscellaneous suggestions: at **Pandit Brothers**, 10 F Connaught Place, you'll find the **crisp pure-cotton "Bombay Dyeing" bed sheets** that nostalgic old India-hands have a soft spot for, and the **Nagaland Emporium** has a great range of dramatic black and red **tribal textiles**, which can be used as wall-hangings or sofa coverings.

Decorative **Rajasthani embroidered wall-hangings and patchwork coverings** are sold by a small cluster of village women **along Janpath** road.

Ceramics and Pottery

Best known among India's many distinctive ceramics is the **blue-glazed pottery** from nearby Khuja in Uttar Pradesh and Jaipur, with its distinctive turquoise and ultramarine floral designs on its white surface. Plates, ash-trays, vases, lamp-bases, soap dishes, door-knobs and buttons – the range is endless – but all are entirely hand-moulded, well-glazed and have a rather Mediterranean look. The best range is found at the **Central Cottage Emporium** on Janpath.

You probably won't have room in your suitcase for them, but it's impossible not to notice how extremely decorative Delhi's ubiquitous ochre-red unglazed terracotta *matkas*, or water pots, might look tucked among your garden plants at home.

Just **outside the New Delhi Railway Station**, there's an open-air market piled high with all sorts of pots, plates, candle-holders and animal-shaped clay wares are bartered. Around the corner, off the main road, look for the *khumba* or **potter's workshop,** where pots are thrown, dried in the sun, splashed with a red wash and placed in a communal kiln.

Papier mâché

The best quality **Kashmiri** *papier mâché* goods are extremely delicate, etched with real gold, not bronze dust or poster paint. The making of *papier mâché* is a laborious process: pulped paper is first soaked in an adhesive fluid, dried in a mold for at least a month, then painted with bright designs before being coated with varnish. Traditionally, only men and boys do this work, and the best factories still use natural extracts for color: coral is ground for red, lapis for blue, charcoal for black and cardamom for yellow. Prices depend on the quality of the design and materials. There are boxes, eggs, paper-holders, egg cups, lamps, coasters and trays. Try browsing in the **Kashmir Government Emporium** along Baba Kharak Singh Marg.

Decorative arts

Among the many collector's items are marble-inlaid pieta dura pieces from Agra, which are made by craftsmen using exactly the same techniques that created the Taj Mahal's intricate surfaces. The most popular *pieta dura* creations are coasters, chess-board, jewelry boxes and table tops.

Crafts from Orissa and Tamil Nadu also deserve a special mention:

specialities include beautiful carved boxes and statues of **soft soap-stone**, as well as vibrant **applique-work** wall-hangings and giant umbrellas. From Gujarat, look for stuffed toys, exotic lacquered swing seats and children's cradles.

Wood carvings

Sandalwood carvings of gods and animals from south India mainly cater to the mass market, and can be found everywhere. In the **Kashmir emporiums**, look for ornately carved **Kashmiri walnut or rosewood furniture**, wooden screens, tables and jewelry boxes, which can be either in natural finish or lacquered.

In the antique shops, you'll find an endless variety of carved statues, textile-blocks and even temple carvings fragments.

Metal art objects

Look especially for **bronze-cast figures** of gods and goddesses – reproductions of original 10th to 12th-century south Indian Chola statues – in all shapes and sizes at **Poompahar (Tamil Nadu) Emporium** on Baba Kharak Singh Marg. The age-old wax-casting method by which they are made has changed little over the centuries: a wax figure is made, a mould formed around it, the wax melted and poured out, so that molten bronze can be poured into the cavity to solidify, and later emerge from the cast as a finished figurine.

Elsewhere you'll see countless **brass statues**, Tibetan *samovars*, Buddhas, *hookah* bases, nut-crackers, dishes and pot-plant holders – all mass-produced and cheap. **Chawri bazaar** is best for serious brass and copper enthusiasts, with many aesthetic domestic utensils.

You'll recognize traditional Hyderabadi *bidri* ware from its distinctive silver designs inlaid on black gunmetal.

Coffee or tea sets made up of 90 percent silver or **"white metal"** – an alloy of copper, zinc and nickel with silver plating are worth buying. Check out the shops along **Janpath**.

Rows of junk and tourist shops on Janpath

In the antique and curio shops you can find anything from life-size brass statues of Hanuman to tiny old betel leaf plates, exquisite bell-metal figurines to intriguing tribal grain measures.

Leather goods

Leatherware is definitely a good buy in India. Because sheep leather and skilled labor is abundant, prices are very low. For leather jackets in **Western styles**, shoes, smart briefcases, handbags, luggage and wallets you'll find the best buys at the Taj Mahal Hotel's **Khazana shop,** and **The Shop** in Regal Building. Quality is better at the former but prices are much better at the latter. If you're lucky you could buy something which looks like it came from Milan, but cost a fraction of the price.

Also look out for Rajasthani *mojadis* or slippers, usually made from camel skin and decorated with embroidered designs. They make fun presents for children, especially the curled-up "Sinbad" style slippers. **Leather sandals** made to Brazilian styles can also be found, and the best place to look is **Janpath's Tibetan Market.**

Ethnic chic boutiques at Haus Khas village

Western clothes

Delhi has hundreds of garment-production factories catering to European fashion houses, and it's possible to pick up **designer seconds** or rejects which are dumped on the market each season at incredibly cheap prices. Sure, sometimes the color runs, or there's a slight defect, but if you have a discerning eye, you'll be surprised at what you can find along **Janpath** and in **Palika Bazaar.**

For fashionable light cottons, try the bone fide Benetton shop at the end of Baba Kharak Singh Marg.

Tea and coffee

India is the world's largest producer of tea, and its most famous leaves are household names. Delhi has three exceptional tea shops, but the best is **Aap ki Pasand Tea Taster's Center** at 15 Netaji Subhash Marg, where you can sample delicious brews and blends of aromatic Darjeeling, Assamese and Orange Pekoe before buying gift-wrapped packages. Otherwise, try **Tea City** at 133 Sarojini Nagar Market, Delhi's only tea "supermarket", and **Mittal Stores** at 12 Sundar Nagar. South Indian coffee is very delicious, packed and sold by the government and very, very cheap. For beans or crushed powder that you can take home, try the **Indian Coffee Board**, at 66 Tolstoy Lane (behind the Lufthansa office in Janpath).

Perfumes

Essential perfume oils, or *attars*, are a major industry in India, and make perfect gifts. Try **R-Expo**, 1115, Main Bazaar, Paharganj, opposite the Big Mosque, for a vast range and aesthetic gift-wrapping in ornate sandalwood holders. Also try Gulab Singh's fascinating, sweet-scented shop in **Dariba Kalan**, and stalls in **Meena Bazaar** or **Nizamuddin village.**

Calendar of Special Events

The Indian calendar brims with hundreds of festivals and many fairs all year round. For its most special days, India explodes with dazzling color, religious pageantry, trumpets, fireworks, tinsel, feasting, glorious costumes, brocade-showered idols, and magic outdoor processions of caparisoned elephants. The dates of most festivals are calculated according to the Indian lunar calendar, and can be determined only by around October the previous year. At this time your nearest Government of India tourist office should have the full list of upcoming festival dates.

January - February

International Film Festival. Held in Delhi on odd years, (1991), another Indian city on evens.

Kite Festival (14th January). Kite-flyers can be seen everywhere on this day, so that the sky flutters with thousands of brightly-colored tissue kites.

Republic Day (26th January), is an important national festival celebrated in all over India, but most spectacular in New Delhi, which stages a magnificent military parade with regiments in full dress, bands, richly caprisoned camels and elephants, floats and colorful folk dancers rolling along Rajpath. It is followed by a two-day festival of music and dance, offering the chance to see exotic folk dances from all over India. Don't take along anything valuable, as all baggage has to be left with security. Buy tickets through the Tourist Office in Janpath.

"Beating the Retreat" (29th January). This solemn and beautiful dusk pageant which follows Republic Day, assembles various sections of the armed forces in a parade that is extremely reminiscent of the British Raj. The Central Secretariat is decorated

The camel cavalry march

with fairy lights, and the camel regiment and cavalry stand on parade forming a magnificent silhouette with Rashtrapai Bhavan as a backdrop.

Vasant Panchami. This festival honors Saraswati, the Hindu goddess of knowledge, and is celebrated with colorful processions and kite-flying, best seen in West Bengal. Paint-brushes, ball-point pens and musical instruments are reverently placed at Saraswati's shrine, as if to encourage continued creativity.

February - March.

Shivrati. This Hindu festival is held in honor of Shiva, the religion's father figure. Devotees fast for a day, then fall upon dates, fruits, nuts, sweet potatoes and rice – Shiva's favorite snack.

Holi. This is India's color-doused version of April Fools day. Spring is celebrated with explosive Bacchanalian, powder-throwing, paint-squirting revelry that breaks down all traditional barriers of caste or religion in an atmosphere of playful flirtation. On the night before, bonfires are lit and a bamboo and straw effigy of the demoness Holika is set ablaze as people dance around the flames.

In Delhi, celebrations are not always as fun as they should be – and unwary foreigners may not enjoy the experience of being sloshed with buckets of paint from rooftop pranksters. Go prepared like everyone else by purchasing plenty of powder, paint and water-pistols, and wear clothes that can be thrown away the next day. Don't despair – you may resemble a walking artist's palette for days, or even weeks later – but the color will eventually come out!

Delhi Horse Show. Show jumping and equestrian feats go on display during this show in mid-February.

Suraj Kund Crafts Mela. 1st-15th February 1991. Craftsmen from all over India gather near the historic 10th- century pool on the outskirts of Delhi for a fortnight's fair and offer a wealth of finished wares to sell.

The Delhi Flower Show. Held at Pragati Maidan and a must for green-fingered enthusiasts. This is followed by the All India Rose Show, which is organized by the Rose Society of India.

March - April

Good Friday and **Easter**. As in the West, these Christian festivals are also observed in India.

Mahavir Jayanti. This Jain festival is dedicated to Mahavira, the 24th Jain Thirthankara or saint, and founder of Jainism, an ascetic religion which stresses non-violence.

Baisakhi. For Hindus, this festival marks the descent of the sacred Ganges river to earth, and devotees throng to

The phallic symbol fo Si

holy rivers (including Delhi's Yamuna) to bathe and worship. Sikhs also celebrate it to commemorate the day in 1689 that Guru Gobind Singh founded the Khalsa or militant brotherhood of the Sikhs, and perform Bhangra dance, as wild and vigorous as the Cossacks.

Ram Navami. Devotees chant prayers and sing ballads to mark the birthday of the Hindu god Rama.

Id-ul-Fitr. Also known as Ramazan-Id, this is a major Muslim celebration which marks the end of Ramazan, the Islamic month of fasting. Thousands of devout Muslims stream into the Jama Masjid to kneel in prayer, then rejoice and feast.

May - June

Buddha Purnima. Buddhists celebrate Buddha's birth, enlightenment and attainment of nirvana all one day, even though these events occurred in different years.

July - August

Raksha Bandhan. Hindu women tie decorative tinsel threads called *rakhi* around the wrists of their brothers to remind them of their duty to protect

their sisters. It commemorates the god Indra's battle victory after his wife gave him a rakhi.

Independence Day on August 15.

Janmashtami. Hindus celebrate the birth of Krishna with feasts and *ras lila* dances after a fast, and make pilgrimage to Krishna temples.

August - September

Muharram. Shi'ite Muslims commemorate the murder in 680 AD of Iman Hussain, the Prophet Muhammed's grandson, with 10 days of mourning. This culminates in a street parade heralded by drums, makeshift floats bearing *tazias* (replicas of Hussain's tomb), and scrums of men engaged in ritual self-flagellation with whips and even razor blades.

September/October

Dussehra. Also known as Navarati or Durga Purga, this major 10-day festival celebrates the god Rama's victory over the Lankan demon Ravanna who had captured his abducted wife Sita, as recounted in the Hindu epic, the *Ramayana.* Continuous plays, marathon readings, music and dance are performed by weird and wonderfully dressed actors on chariots in Chandhi Chowk. The festival culminates in a procession of immense firework-padded, brightly painted effigies of the evil ten-headed Ravana and his henchmen to Delhi's Ram Lila fairground where they are set ablaze to the cheers of thousands of onlookers.

Ready to play the part of Ram during the Dussehra festival

October - November

Diwali. This so-called "festival of lights" traditionally takes place on the full moon night after Dussehra. It's the gayest and most riotous of all Indian festivals, with a night-long display of fireworks, illuminations and general pageantry. Throughout India, houses are cleaned and repainted to honor Lakshmi, the goddess of wealth and the home, then bedecked with hundreds of oil lamps.

Mahatma Gandhi's Birthday (2 October).

November

Nanak Jayanti. Sikhs celebrate the birthday of their founder, Guru Nanak with prayers and processions.

December

Christmas (December 25th). Christians celebrate Christ's birthday with a special mass.

What to Know?
Practical Information

TRAVEL ESSENTIALS

Arrival

The **Indira Gandhi International Airport** lies a **30-minute drive southwest of central Delhi** and has an international and domestic terminal. While airport facilities have improved considerably in recent years, long queues and delays in baggage collection are still common. Jet-lagged newcomers usually land in Delhi during the early hours of the morning – the arrival and departure time of most international flights.

Recent political extremism in India has led to greatly enhanced security, and do not be surprised if even after you have cleared customs, your bags are run through an X-ray machine. Money changing and hotel-booking facilities are located within the airport complex.

Emerging from the air-conditioned airport, most travelers are instantly enveloped by waves of sticky heat and pungent, unfamiliar scents from the darkness – and unsteadily step into what seems a flickering throng of shouting Indians, bundle-like pavement sleepers, car horns bleeping in unison and taxi touts pulling at your shirt sleeves. Stay cool and collected, and discourage touts with a firm "no thank you" and they'll leave you alone. Unless you are desperate for a porter, it's best to keep a firm grip on all your personal belongings; a small Rs5 tip per trolley of luggage is ample.

If you are not being met and need a taxi, make a beeline for the **Pre-Paid Taxi Counter** before leaving the airport, which organizes a taxi to your hotel at a fixed rate; this avoids jumping into the deep end with bartering in an unknown city. Alternatively there are airport-to-city buses. A ride into the city center should cost about Rs80.

When to visit

Delhi is at its most comfortable between October to February, when the days are pleasantly crisp and sunny, with daytime temperatures of around 71.5°F (22°C), and cool evenings.

December and January are decidedly chilly, with nightime lows of 39°F (4°C). Winter is also Delhi's wedding season – a good time for seeing spontaneous processions of brocade-clad turbanned grooms on white horses and their glittering brides with an *entourage* of drunken guests, lamp-*wallahs* and epauletted bandsmen.

Delhi has a fleeting, but beautiful blossoming splendor during the spring months of February and March, when wide avenues and lush parks brim with riotous flowers.

The searing summer months of May and June are oppressively hot, with the mercury soaring to daytime highs of 114°F (46°C) so that air-conditioning is essential. More than one executive traveler has resorted to conducting business in a hotel pool. Unpredictable dust storms often send silty squalls from Rajasthan's desert plains across the capital, sometimes disrupting internal flights. It's best to start the day early, take a long afternoon siesta from noon to 3 or 4 p.m., then venture out again. With recent monsoons so erratic, the searing heat of May and July may or may not be relieved by the life-giving rains of July and August.

September can be humid, with occasional downpours, but it is usually pretty and green.

Visas

A **tourist visa** is required for all visitors to India, and it is absolutely imperative to receive clearance from

India's local embassy before departing. Immigration officials steadfastly refuse to allow entry to anyone without proper documentation, and most airlines check the passports for all India-destined passengers as they have in the past borne the cost of numerous deported travelers.

Apply well in advance as visas usually take about two weeks to clear. Indian officials usually grant a 120-day stay, and charge the reciprocal equivalent of what your nation charges for Indians to enter. You can apply for an extension or a re-entry permit at the Foreigners Registration Office, Hans Bhawan, Indraprastra Estate, tel: 3318179, 3319489 (near the Tilak Bridge Railway Station).

Vaccinations

No vaccination is required for entry into India. But a valid certificate of vaccination is required for those coming from yellow fever infected areas (mostly South and Central America and Africa) is required.

A pot-pourri of vaccinations is recommended against cholera, typhoid, tetanus, hepatitis A and polio, as well as a course of malaria tablets.

Have your injections at least a fortnight before departing, so that the immunizations have time to take full effect and you can recover from any lingering reaction.

Cholera vaccines remain active for six months. The vaccine against hepatitis A, gamma globulin, is effective for two months, so those intending a longer stay should ask for a double dose.

Customs

Visitors are allowed to carry in one duty-free bottle of spirits and 200 cigarettes. Foreigners can bring any amount of foreign currency or traveler's checks into India, provided they declare the amount of checks on arrival in the Currency Declaration Form. Cash, bank notes and traveler's checks up to US$1,000 need not be declared. No Indian currency, with the exception of rupee traveler's checks, are permitted to be taken out of India.

Prohibited articles include the import of gold and silver bullion, and the Indian government imposes strict regulations to check this – dangerous drugs and live plants.

Video cameras must also be declared, and must again be produced when leaving the country.

Other dutiable items such as electronic goods and jewelry can be imported duty-free as long as they are taken out of the country when you leave. For this, you may need to complete a **Tourist Baggage Re-Export Form (TBRE),** prepared by a customs officer. The TBRE must be retained and submitted along with departure from the country along with proof that items entered on it are re-exported.

Money matters

Currency is based on the decimal system with 100 *paise* to the rupee, which is available in denominations of 1, 2, 5, 10, 20, 50, 100 and 500. Avoid swapping hard currency on the black market; there are serious penalties for offenders and the consequences rarely match the unofficial exchange rate, usually a mere 10-20 percent above what government banks are offering.

Exchanging cash and traveler's checks can be a rigmarole, involving endless forms and being referred to at least four different officers before you get the money in your pocket. For this reason, it is often best to change sizable sums of money to minimize time spent on such consuming procedures. Your passport is essential identification for changing money, and generally traveler's checks have a better rate than cold cash.

Rupee notes are often delivered in bundles stapled and sealed as protection against corruption, and it can be difficult to change a 100 rupee note on the street, so it is wise to change some at the bank so you have small change for rickshaws, tips and fending off persistent street urchins.

There is also a reluctance to accept any bills slightly ripped or worn, so be careful your change does not include notes that will prove difficult to get rid of. Banks and five-star hotels will graciously accept this exhausted currency.

Credit cards have found widespread acceptance at shops and restaurants and you will find the American Express and Visa logos virtually everywhere.

While plastic is a convenient way of reserving travel funds, most private shopkeepers will try and charge you the percentage that they are meant to pay the card company. It is rare to be able to persuade wily traders out of this uncharitable state of mind, and be prepared to pay 3 percent for American Express, and 6 percent for credit cards such as Visa and Diners Club.

However, the plastic is advantageous when paying in five-star hotels, they drop a 20 percent "luxury tax" for food, victuals and accommodation if you are paying with foreign currency.

Foreigners are generally required to use hard currency to settle accounts at hotels, but can use rupees if they present an encashment certificate proving the source of their local currency was an official bank. This system is pretty sham, and you can repeatedly use the same certificate which may not have any correlation to the rupees you are spending at all.

Clothing

For most of the year, the most practical clothing for India should be loose cotton or natural fibers that allow your skin to breathe.

Make sure you read the international temperature guide in your local newspaper before arriving in Delhi, and plan your wardrobe accordingly.

In the winter months of December to February, make sure you come prepared with woollens and jackets.

Essential items in your luggage include socks for visiting temples or mosques (to avoid hot marble or tiles), slip-on sandals or shoes to go with them, hat and sunglasses for sightseeing and a bathing costume for cooloing off in hotel pools.

Electricity

Electrical outlets are rated at 220 volts, 50 cycles and accept round-pronged plugs, so check to see if you need to buy an adapter for your hair dryer, travel iron or shaver.

Airport tax

A tax of Rs 300 is charged at the airport on departure. If you are going to neighboring countries such as Nepal, Pakistan, Sri Lanka, the Maldives and Bangladesh, the charge is Rs 150.

GETTING ACQUAINTED

Geography

India, with a population of 850 million people, covers a total area of 1,270,000 sq miles (3,287,782 sq km), approximately the size of Europe. Nearly 80 percent of its population live in villages, engaged in subsistence farming. India is primarily an agricultural nation, but it also one of the world's largest industrial powers with major iron and steel production and a growing manufacturing industry, particularly for export textiles.

The capital of India comprises old Delhi, (built by the Mughal rulers) and New Delhi, (built by the British). The city lies west of the Yamuna river. The Union Territory of New Delhi and its suburbs cover 368 sq miles (1,489 sq km). It has a population of 7.8 million by 1988 estimates. It lies on India's Indo-Ganges plain between neighboring Uttar Pradesh, Haryana and Punjab states.

Agra, home of the Taj Mahal, is 126 miles (203 km) south of Delhi. It bears the imprint of the Mughal rulers who turned it into a city of monuments. Agra is one of the key cities of Uttar Pradesh. It measures about 23 sq miles (62 sq km) and has a population of about 800,000.

Climate

The seasons are divided as follows, with daytime temperatures given:

Hot Season
March to June: 88°-105°F`(30°-41°C)

Monsoon Season
June to September: 105°-93°F (41°-34°C)

Cool Season
November to February: 53°-75°F (12°-24°C)

Time

Indian Standard Time is 5½ hours ahead of Greenwich Mean Time and 9½ hours ahead of US EST. However, time is a very elastic concept in India. Indeed in Hindi, the same word is used to describe "yesterday" and "tomorrow".

How not to offend

If you're in Delhi on a business trip or are meeting up with friends, you'll find your Indian contacts will go out of their way to help you. You'll probably be invited home, where Indian good humor and hospitality flow if you prove congenial company. Overwhelming personal generosity can be thanked by flowers bought on the spot, which florists make into beautiful bouquets for little or no cost, or a bottle of Scotch whisky brought in the suitcase.

When invited to dinner, expect to eat late, at around 10 p.m., after a long pre-dinner interval of drinks and yet more drinks.

Hindus do not eat beef, which is not sold legally in India, and Muslims shun pork. Many Hindus are also vegetarians, an important point to remember when you ask Indians out to dinner.

To avoid upsetting locals, low-cut necklines, high-cut hemlines and very short shorts are best worn inside the hotel only, and never (never!) in holy places. Bikinis are fine at the hotel pool. If you're a women, you'll find it pays to dress in comfortable, but concealing garments to deflect obvious admirers.

Whom do you trust?

Although Delhi might strike some visitors as an alarming place, it is fairly safe. You might feel conspicuous as a westerner, (*feringhi*) but you're not so rare: Delhi has a large community of foreign diplomats, business people and journalists as well as its seasonal surge of tourists.

Because many Indians tend to be gregarious, sometimes almost embarrassingly so, it can be difficult, even for long-time foreign residents, to discern whether apparent kindness is in fact merely devised to somehow persuade you to part with your rupees.

In general, it's best not to trust anyone who sidles up alongside you to start a conversation, especially in central areas such as Connaught Place, where opportunists are rife.

Although taxi-drivers and commission-seeking touts will often try to fleece you, you'll find most Indians you encounter surprisingly honest.

It's wise to place your valuables in your hotel's locker for safekeeping, or wear a money-belt beneath your clothes to deflect pick-pockets. Generally, you should have no fear of being mugged or attacked during the day, either along the broad avenues of New Delhi, or within the alleys of old Delhi, although as with any city, it's best to have your wits about you.

Delhi's north-Indian Punjabi settlers are largely responsible for "eve-teasing", or female harassment. After the sun sets, it's not wise for lone women to go out strolling in any part of the city or to drive alone late at night, unlike the more cosmopolitan and busy city of Bombay.

Affluent private homes have day/ night watchmen, window-grilles, large fences and often private guards installed in the wake of the horrific 1984 communal riots sparked off by Indira Gandhi's assassination, and a grim reminder of what can happen in times of national strife.

Tipping

Paying with plastic is advantageous when in luxury hotels or higher-class restaurants who drop a 20 percent "luxury tax" for food, victuals and accommodation if you are paying with foreign currency.

Tipping is expected, but the amount varies with the occasion. At a five-star hotel, an exceptionally vigilant waiter could be tipped Rs 100, while at a modest eating house, Rs 10 would be considered generous.

Tourist Information

The main **Government of India Tourist Office** is at 88 Janpath (tel: 332-0005, 332-0342). Helpful staff can advise on your travel plans and have pamphlets. You can also pick up a useful, and free, **map of Delhi**.

The **Delhi Tourism Development Corporation** is at N-Block Connaught Circus, (tel: 331-3637, 331-5322).

In **Agra**, there's a tourist office at **191 The Mall** (tel: 72-377) opposite the General Post Office. All offices are open from 9 a.m. to 5.30 p.m. from Monday to Friday, and from 9 a.m. to 1 p.m. on Saturday, closed on all national holidays.

Of several information publications about Delhi, the best are *Delhi Diary* and *Invitation New Delhi*, offered free at hotels, which give current information on events and cultural attractions.

GETTING AROUND

Few visitors to Delhi fail to be astounded by the anarchic haphazardness of the capital's driving, where a combination of relatively well-paved roads and strident Darwinian aggression constantly prove fatal.

According to statistics, Delhi's roads are among the most dangerous in the world, and there seems every indication that they will stay that way. You'll need to adopt a little Hindu fatalism to stay cool. Even so, expect to have a few near-misses with lurching, over-crammed sardine-can buses or snail's-pace motor-scooters, atop which an entire family have arranged themselves. Only a few self-drive hire cars are available, and it would be madness to drive yourself.

If you decide to head off on foot, you'll find that Delhi is very spread out – so that you can easily feel that you've spent most of your time just getting from one place to another. However, the Connaught Place/Janpath business district is compact enough, and a sweat-inducing 30-minute trek should take you anywhere you need to go.

Finding your way

New Delhi's grid-like sweeping boulevards and concentric rings are relatively easy for you to find your way around – roads are well signed and all the street names uniformly belong to the post-Independence era.

When venturing out into Delhi's suburban "colonies" however, residential or business addresses can be devilish to find; always seek advance directions, and mark them out on your map, also make sure you foray forth armed with the telephone number of your host.

It's also helpful to ask the name of the nearest cinema as a landmark – since taxi and auto drivers are inveterate movie-goers and will be able to make a beeline for your destination.

Expect police check-points in unlikely, unlit spots at night, but foreigners are usually waved on immediately since the real prey are terrorists.

Rental cars

A hired car or limousine (air-conditioned with a driver) is best arranged either through your hotel or an agent (eg. SITA World Travel, F12 Connaught Place, tel: 316-514, 316-663 Budget, tel: 371-5657, Hertz, tel: 331-8695, 331-0190). You can get a list of approved car operators from the Tourist Information Office. A one-day hire of an air-conditioned, chauffeured taxi costs about Rs350.

Taxis

Taxis are easily recognised by their bumble-bee yellow tops and black bodies, and can be hired from most hotels and numerous stands. The vehicle will either be the inveterate Ambassador, a clunking 1957 Morris Oxford still produced in India, or the Padmini, a zippier 1950s model Fiat.

Drivers will wait quite happily if you want to retain them, while you hive off for an hour of so of sightseeing or shopping. Their meter should work, the tip is 10 percent, plus waiting time of about Rs10 per hour, and an extra 25 percent "night charge" between 11 p.m. and 5 a.m.

Drivers will often insist their meter is not working as they wish to charge more – so always agree on a price first (this deflects the driver's inclination to waste his petrol driving you in circles).

Sternly deflect any driver's offers to buy your cameras, whisky, or foreign currency; be discreet about changing money on the black market in Delhi, since many drivers are police informers.

Auto-rickshaws

While you'll probably never really enjoy them, auto-rickshaws provide the cheapest, most convenient way of negotiating short distances. But they are totally impractical for longer distances like to the airport or to the Qutb Minar for not only do they rattle your kidneys, they constantly break down as their insides are usually held together by bits of wire. Most have meters; otherwise, fixed sums should work out at less than half the taxi rate.

Rickshaws

In old Delhi, you can get about the bazaars by man-powered bicycle rickshaw, which seats one to two – and has no noise, no petrol fumes, only *chapati* power! Rates should be agreed on in advance; big bottoms should pay tips!

Buses

The city buses are strictly for the courageous or destitute, especially during the rush hour, when there seem as many people hanging desperately off the sides as sandwiched inside.

Tours

City Tours in Delhi are conducted by the Delhi Tourism Development Corporation (DTDC) at N-36 Bombay Life Building, Connaught Place (tel: 331-3637), and the Indian Tourism Development Corporation (ITDC), L-Block, Connaught Circus (tel: 350-331). Both provide half, full-day or evening tours. The ITDC tours are better at Rs30 for half-day and Rs60 for a full day tour.

One-day tours of the Taj Mahal, Agra Fort and Fatehpur Sikri are conducted by the UP State Tourist Development Corporation at Taj Khema, Eastern Gate, Taj Mahal (tel: 653-383) and the UP State Rd Transport Corporation, 96 Gwalior Rd (tel: 72-206).

Full-day tours begin at 10.15 a.m. and end at 6.30 p.m., cost Rs40 and are devised for day-trippers from Delhi who need to be back at Agra Station in time to catch the Shatabdi Express.

Maps

Maps of Delhi can be obtained free from the Tourist Office on Janpath, or purchased in bookshops or from street vendors everywhere.

Accurate, excellent maps of India can be obtained from the map section of the Survey of India office, next to the Cottage Industries Emporium on Janpath. Otherwise, ask for Bartholomew's map of India and the subcontinent at any bookshop.

WHERE TO STAY

Hotels

Delhi is one of India's busiest entry points for foreign visitors, expatriates and business people. It has a fleet of 5-star international-class luxury hotels, all modern, with top-notch restaurants, 24-hour coffee shops, swimming pools (a definite must during summer), business desks, travel agents, shopping arcades and even in-house astrologers.

It's always essential to advance-book 5-star accommodation in Delhi, especially during the peak-season months between October and March.

Visitors should not expect subcontinental "shoe-string" prices. Although accommodation is still relatively cheap by international standards, five-star hotels are rapidly catching up. All rates are subject to 10 percent tax.

All hotels mentioned below take American Express, and bills must be settled in foreign currency, or on production of a Cash Encashment Certificate from a bank, with rupees which you can prove you have purchased.

Expensive

Approx. Rs1,500 - 2,200

The Oberoi
Dr Zakir Hussain Marg,
Te: 363-030
(City center).

Taj Mahal Hotel
1 Mansingh Rd,
Tel: 301-6162
(City center).

Welcomgroup Maurya Sheraton
Sardar Patel Marg

Diplomatic Enclave
Tel: 301-0101
(Chanakyapuri).

Taj Palace Intercontinental Hotel
2 Sardar Patel Marg,
Diplomatic Enclave,
Tel: 301-0404,
(Chanakyapuri).

Hyatt Regency
Bhikaji Cama Place
Tel: 609-911
(Mid-way between Airport and city center)

Holiday Inn
Connaught Plaza
Tel: 332-0101
(Inner city).

Le Meridien Hotel
Windsor Place
Janpath
Tel: 389-821
(Inner City).

Approx. Rs1,000 - 1,800

Centaur Hotel
Tel: 545-2223
(Airport)

Ashok Hotel
50-B Chanakyapuri
Tel: 600-412
(City center)

Moderate

Approx. Rs800 -1200

Several impeccable 'colonial' hotels offer less expensive elegance with plenty of period flair as well as efficiency:

Hotel Imperial
Janpath
Tel: 332-4540
(Inner city)

Clandges
12 Aurangzeb Rd
Tel: 301-0211
(City center)

Oberoi Maidens
7 Sham Nath Marg
Tel: 252-5464
(Civil Lines, near Old Delhi)

Modest

Approx. Rs600 - 900

Hotel Ambassador
Sujan Singh Park
Tel: 690-391
(City center)

Lodhi Hotel
Lala Lajpat Rai Marg
Tel: 619-422
(City Center)

Rs700 and below

Ashok Yatri Niwas (ITDC)
19 Ashok Road
Tel: 332-4511
(Inner City)

Marina Hotel
G-59, Connaught Place
Tel: 344-658
(Inner City)

Nirula's Hotel
L Block,Connaught Place
Tel: 352-419
(Inner City)

YMCA Tourist Hostel
Jai Singh Road
Tel: 311-915
(Inner City)

YWCA International Guest House
Parliament Street (Sansad Marg)
Tel: 311-561
(Inner City)

Blue Triangle Family Hostel
Ashoka Road
Tel: 310-133
(Inner City)

Guest houses

There are a number of small, cheap guest houses suitable for the **budget traveler**. They are located around **Janpath** and in **Paharganj** near the New Delhi Railway Station. Prices range from Rs50 to Rs100. Government-run tourist camps also provide these facilities. Enquiries can be made at the **tourist office on Janpath**.

More expensive guest houses with better facilities are located in smart residential areas.

The following are recommended:

Maharani Guest House
3 Sunder Nagar
Tel: 693-128
(City Center)

Jukaso Inn
50 Sunder Nagar
Tel: 69-0308

Manor House
77 Friends Colony West
Tel: 683-2171
(South Delhi)

HOURS OF BUSINESS AND PUBLIC HOLIDAYS

Business hours

Offices and shops are generally open from 10 a.m. to 5 p.m. every day except Sundays. Banks function between 10 a.m. and 2 p.m. on Monday to Friday, and 10 a.m. to noon on Saturdays.

Most hotels can change traveler's checks, and post mail for you, selling the stamps at reception.

Public holidays

The following days are observed as public holidays during 1990 and 1991. The dates for Hindu, Sikh and Jain festivals vary with the lunar calendar, although keeping to roughly fixed times, and can only be determined by around October of the previous year.

Muslim festivals sometimes move right round the year.

Republic Day: January 26

Holi: March 1, 1991

Mahavir Jayanti: March 28, 1991

Good Friday: April 13, 1990

Ramzan Id (Id-Ul-Fitr): April 17, 1991

May Day: May 1

Bakri Id (Id-Ul-Zuha): June 23, 1991

Muharram: July 23, 1991

Independence Day: August 15

Dussehra: September 23-29, 1990,

October 18, 1991

Gandhi Jayanti: October 2

Diwali: October 18,1990, November 5, 1991

Guru Nanak's Birthday: November 5, 1990, November 21, 1991

Christmas: December 25

HEALTH AND EMERGENCY

Adjust to the highly-spiced Indian diet slowly, sticking to fairly bland dishes like rice, yoghurt, breads and boiled eggs the first couple of days of arrival. In general, it is risky to eat street food prepared by pavement vendors, raw vegetables, unpeeled or unsterilized fruits and food with a high water content, such as lettuce, tomatoes and watermelon.

India has a fantastic array of vegetarian dishes and many travelers avoid red meats and pork as these can contain nasty parasites. Poultry is usually safe. Seafood is best eaten in coastal regions, but Delhi's main hotels are also generally safe.

However, you must not be overly fastidious or you will miss sampling the remarkable fare India offers. Food freshly cooked and sold straight from the brazier at roadside *dhabas*, or cafes, is delicious and usually safe.

The best rule is to eat at places with a high turnover so that food served is usually fresh. Ironically, five-star hotels often produce tummy troubles as these serve food with sauces and dressings such as mayonnaise that are best left alone. Be sensible, if something looks or smells borderline, do not eat it. In smaller restaurants, it is best to wash your hands before chowing down.

If you are smitten by diarrhea or any gippy tummy, treat all spiced oily foods as taboo. Eat sparing amounts of bland boiled rice, yoghurt and bananas, and drink plenty of black tea and boiled water. It is best to try and work the bugs out of your system, but if your travel itinerary demands an immediate calmed stomach, take some Lomotol tablets to halt diarrhea.

Avoid immediately taking antibiotics as these will kill the bugs, but also any other bacterial resistance you have accumulated, making you susceptible to a second bout.

If problems persist for more than two days, particularly if accompanied by fever, consult a doctor as you may be suffering from dysentery, an illness that will require medical treatment.

Emergency

Most hotels have house physicians who can attend to complaints or recommend a specialist or hospital. Medicines are available at chemist shops either in the hotel or in shopping centers. The chemist shops at Super Bazaar in Connaught Place and All India Medical Institute are open 24 hours.

Hospitals

All India Institute of Medical Science (AIIMS), Ansari Nagar, Sri Aurobindo Marg, tel: 661-123, and **Ram** **Manohar Lohia Hospital at Baba Kharak Singh Marg** (tel: 345-525) are reputable hospitals.

Of Delhi's private clinics, **East West Medical Centre**, 38 Golf Links, tel: 699-229 and the **Ashlok Clinic**, (behind Kamal Cinema), Safdarjung Enclave, are among the best.

Dental clinics

Try **Dr. Siddharth Mehta**, Khan Market, tel: 694-042, 615-914, **Dr. R.K. Bali**, E-13 East of Kailash, tel: 643-1012, **Dr. Mukesh Jetley**, C-225 Defence Colony, tel: 621-097, or **Dr. Pavan Khurana,** B-45, Greater Kailash I, tel: 643-4315

Some useful telephone numbers

Police: 100

Fire Brigade: 101

Ambulance: 102

COMMUNICATIONS AND NEWS

Telecommunications

Telephone systems, unlike water and electricity supplies, tend to run fairly efficiently in upmarket neighborhoods and large hotels. Otherwise, getting through on local or long-distance calls can be a matter of luck. The old maxim: if at first you don't succeed, try, try again, has a special ring to it here.

If you're staying at a five-star hotel, it's quite easy to make calls internationally or long-distance within India by direct dialing. Otherwise, calls must be made through an operator from crowded booths at the local post office.

A word of caution for those who spend much of their time in their hotel bedrooms making either domestic or international calls. Hotels usually whack on stiff service charges for this service, so it is worth checking their terms before you begin a calling binge.

Fax facilities have yet to make an impact in India. Most five-star hotels have business centers with fax services, but rates tend to be pricey at Rs260 per page, plus an additional 10 percent service charge for a fax to an international destination.

Filing information by a computer modem through a telephone line can be erratic as one line hit will disrupt the data flow, but usually after two or three times the message is received at the other end.

Postal services

Mail Services in India are generally good, although it's best to watch staff franking your letter to ensure that the stamp is not immediately peeled off and resold – a common practice.

Sending a parcel abroad can be a complicated and time-consuming business. Either bear with excess luggage or get government emporia to ship your shopping home.

The New Delhi Poste Restante is located in Bhai Veer Singh Marg, off Baba Kharak Singh Marg close to Connaught Place. But beware: Delhi Post Office (as opposed to New Delhi) is near Kashmiri Gate, north of the Red Fort, so make sure your correspondents known which one to send your mail to.

News media

The daily English newspapers are written in a dense Edwardian prose packed with remarkable colloquialisms, and soon become an addictive beginning to the day if you wish to understand complex Indian politics.

The Times of India is the largest in circulation, and along with *The Statesman of Calcutta* plots a centrist path. *The Indian Express* is anti-government and prone to printing glaring exposés on its front page. *The Hindu* of Madras has a strong science section and solid coverage of southern India, while the *Hindustan Times* is pro-Congress. *The Telegraph, The Independent* and the newly-created *India Post* are more upbeat, with solid feature and photography sections.

You can find major foreign newspapers at your hotel newsagent, but all will be at least a day old when they go on the stands. Local newspapers also advertise ongoing cultural events, but the coverage is haphazard. Major cities usually have a weekly journal dedicated to events, such as *Delhi Diary*.

Sunday newspapers contain matrimonial columns that illustrate how Indian marriages are frequently transactions based on pragmatic assessment. For women, a "wheatish complexion" is an asset, and both sexes are rated by their caste, profession, income and prospects.

More indepth coverage is found in news magazines such as *The Illustrated Weekly* or *Sunday magazine*. But the best read is *India Today*, a fortnightly publication with well-written and researched articles covering all aspects of Indian life.

Television and radio

The electronic media and All India Radio and the two-channel Doordarshan television network are notoriously dull (politicians planting trees, or cricket matches.) Television does have its high points, notably a recent trend toward putting on soap operas based on Hindu epics. The programs enjoy a massive following, with entire villages watching a television set garlanded and blessed for the weekly showing.

India has the world's largest film industry, annually churning out more than 1,000 movies, compared with Hollywood's paltry 400. The industry is centered in Madras and Bombay, and the finished products to the Western eye usually resemble 1940s pantomime of heros, villains, and damsels in distress bursting into song between gun battles.

Cinema has been seriously undermined by the rise of the video. Cassettes are available across the country, incredibly with the most up-to-date Western titles as films are pirated and appear in India within weeks of their release in the United States or Europe.

SPECIAL INFORMATION

Sports facilities

Nearly all large hotels have swimming pools, and all five-star hotels have fitness clubs. At some hotels, you can use the pool even if you aren't staying at the hotel, for a fee of about Rs60 at most hotels, but not the Oberoi Intercontinental or the Taj Mahal which reserves that right exclusively for its guests.

Jogging: The most pleasant place to go jogging is the leafy **Lodhi Gardens**, where the track circles beautiful 11th-century tombs and bamboo groves. Nehru Park, near Chanakyapuri, is larger but is sparse and less appealing.

Golf: The prestigious Delhi Golf Club, **Dr. Zakir Hussain Marg**, tel: 699-239/361-236, is one of the social

fixtures for Delhi's elite. It's open from dawn to 5 p.m. Very beautiful, enclosing two crumbling Lodhi-style tombs. There is an 18 hole championship course and a 9-hole practice course. Non-members can make a down-payment of US$20 during weekdays, and US$25 on weekends, with an additional Rs15 charge for a complete golf set (except balls, which can be purchased at the club shop) and Rs20 for caddy hire.

Polo: *Chukas*, or polo sets, are played daily during the official season between October and March at the club's forest clearing grounds in the Presidents Estate. Very popular with Indian army types and resident diplomats. Non-members are not admitted. Enquiries can be made at tel: 301-5604.

Presidents Estate Polo Club, Rashtrapati Bhavan, tel: 301-5604.

Riding: Delhi's riding clubs are open only to members, and it's practical to go for a canter if you are a friend of a resident member, in which case charges are minimal. If you wish to make enquiries, three clubs are listed below:

Captain Kundan Singh's Delhi Riding Club, Safdarjung Rd., tel: 301-1891.

Tennis: The **Delhi Lawns Tennis Association**, Africa Ave., tel: 653-955/666-140 is open from 6 a.m. to 3 p.m., and has three public courts. Courts can be rented by the hour for Rs50, depending on availability. Hiring a coach costs Rs100-150 per hour.

Gliding: Delhi Gliding Club, Safdarjung Airport, tel: 611-298, open from 3 p.m. to sunset daily. It offers "joyride" flights in Indian-made Pushpaks or US-made Cessna 152s for a very cheap Rs8 per flight, but you have to become a member first at Rs265. You'll be accompanied by an instructor.

USEFUL ADDRESSES

Banks

Banks are open from 10 a.m. to 2 p.m. Monday to Friday, and from 10 a.m. to 12 p.m. on Saturday. They remain closed on all national holidays. The **Central Bank at Hotel Ashok** and the **State Bank at the airport** are open **24 hours**. Most major international banks have branches in New Delhi.

American Express
Hamilton House,
A-block Connaught Place
Tel: 332-7178/332-4119

Bank of America,
Hansalaya Building,
Barakhamba Road
Tel: 331-3833/331-4898

Bank of Tokyo
Jeevan Vihar Building,
Parliament Street
Tel: 341-035/345-105

Banque Nationale de Paris
Hansalaya Building,
Barakhamba Road
Tel: 331-833/331-4898

Citibank
Jeevan Bharati Building,
124 Connaught Circus
Tel: 331-1116

Grindlays Bank
H-10 Connaught Circus,
Tel: 332-3735

Hong Kong and Shanghai Bank
ECE House,
Kasturba Gandhi Marg
Tel: 331-4355/331-4359

The Standard Chartered Bank
17 Parliament Street
Tel: 331-0195

Thomas Cook
Imperial Hotel,
Tel: 332-2171/332-8432

Airline offices

For **international flight information** call 301-7733 and for **domestic flight information** call 545-2434 or 301-4433 (Pre-recorded). (* airport tel:)

Indira Gandhi International Airport,
tel: 394-021/545-2011/301-4433/545-2181

Palam Domestic Airport,
tel: 545-2121/545-2125/393-535

Aeroflot Soviet Airlines
BMC House, 1st Floor
N-1 Connaught Place
Tel: 331-0426/331-2843/*548-2331

Air France
Ashoka Hotel,
Chanakyapuri
Tel: 604-691
or
Scindia House,
Janpath
Tel: 331-0407/*545-2099

Air India
Jeevan Bharati Building
124 Connaught Place
Tel: 331-1225/*545-2050

Air Lanka
Hotel Imperial,
Janpath
Tel: 344-965

Alitalia
Surya Kiran Building,
19 Kasturba Gandhi Marg
Tel: 331-1020/331-1019/*393-140

British Airways
1A Connaught Place
Tel: 332-7428/*545-2077

Indian Airlines
Kanchenchunga Building,
Barakhamba Road
Tel: 331-0052

Cathay Pacific
123 Tolstoy House,
Tolstoy Marg
Tel: 332-2919

Emirates
Kanchenchunga Building,
18 Barakhamba Road
Tel: 331-4529/*548-2861

Gulf Air
G-12 Connaught Place
Tel: 332-7814/*544-2065

Japan Airlines
Chandralok Building,
36 Janpath
Tel: 332-4922/*545-2082

KLM
Prakash Deep Building,
Tolstoy Marg
Tel: 331-5841/331-5844/*394-021

Kuwait Airways
Hansalaya Building,
Barakhamba Road
Tel: 331-4221

Lot Polish Airlines
G-55 Connaught Place
Tel: 332-4221/*544-2295

Lufthansa
56 Janpath
Tel: 332-7268/*545-2062

Pan Am
Chandralok Building,
36 Janpath
Tel: 332-5222/*545-2093

PIA
Kailash Building,
26 Kasturba Gandhi Marg
Tel: 331-3161/*545-2011

Quantas
Room 4, Hotel Janpath
Tel: 332-9732/332-9027

Royal Nepal Airlines
44 Janpath
Tel: 332-1572/*545-3876

Singapore Airlines
G-11 Connaught Place
Tel: 332-0145/*545-2011

SAS
B-1, Connaught Place
Tel: 392-526/*392-672

Swiss Air
56 Janpath
Tel: 332-0145

Thai International
12A Connaught Place
Tel: 332-3638/*548-3898

Vayudoot
Malhotra Building,
F-Block, Janpath
Tel: 331-2587/*545-2313

Travel agencies

SITA World Travel
F12 Connaught Place
Tel: 331-1133, 331-1122

Mercury Travels
4 A Ground Floor,
Jeevan Tara Building,
Parliament Street
Tel: 312-167

American Express,
A Block, Connaught Place
Tel: 344-119, 332-4119

Cox and Kings
Indra Palace,
Connaught Place
Tel: 332-0067

Narula Travels
Mezzanine Floor,
Mohan Dev Building,
13 Tolstoy Marg, New Delhi
Tel: 332-9596, 332-8360.

Diplomatic missions

Australian High Commission
1/50 G ShantiPath,
Chanakyapuri-21
Tel: 601-336

Austrian Embassy
EP13 Chandra Gupta Marg,
Chanakyapuri-21
Tel: 601-112

Bangladesh High Commission
56 Mahatma Gandhi Marg,
Lajpat Nagar-III
Tel: 683-4668

Belgian Embassy
50 Chanakyapuri-21
Tel: 607-957

Brazilian Embassy
8 Aurangzeb Road
Tel: 301-7301

British High Commission
Shantipath,
Chanakyapuri
Tel: 601-371

Burmese Embassy
3/50 Nyaya Marg,
Chanakyapuri
Tel: 600-251

Canadian High Commission
Shantipath,
Chanakyapuri
Tel: 608-161

Chinese Embassy
50D Shantipath,
Chanakyapuri
Tel: 600-328

Danish Embassy
2 Golf Links
Tel: 616-273

Finnish Embassy
Nyaya Marg,
Chanakyapuri
Tel: 605-409

French Embassy
2/50E Shantipath,
Chanakyapuri
Tel: 604-004

German Embassy
6/50G Shanti Path,
Chanakyapuri
Tel: 604-861

Greek Embassy
16 Sunder Nagar
Tel: 617-800

Indonesian Embassy
50A Chanakyapuri
Tel: 602-352

Irish Embassy
13 Jorbagh
Tel: 617-435

Italian Embassy
13 Golf Links
Tel: 618-311

Japanese Embassy
Plot 450G,
Chanakyapuri
Tel: 604-071

Korean Embassy
9 Chandragupta Marg,
Chanakyapuri
Tel: 601-601

Kuwait Embassy
5A Shanti Path,
Chanakyapuri
Tel: 600-791

Laotian Embassy
20 Jorbagh
Tel: 616-187

Mexican Embassy
B-10 Jorbagh
Tel: 697-991

Malaysian High Commission
50M Satya Marg,Chanakyapuri
Tel: 601-291

Mauritian High Commission
5 Kautilya Marg,
Chanakyapuri
Tel: 301-1112

Nepalese Embassy
Barakhamba Road
Tel: 332-9969

Netherlands Embassy
6/50F Shanti Path,
Chanakyapuri
Tel: 609-571

New Zealand High Commission
25 Golf Links
Tel: 697-296

Norwegian Embassy
Shanti Path,
Chanakyapuri
Tel: 605-982

Pakistan High Commission
2/50G Shanti Path,
Chanakyapuri
Tel: 600-601/600-603

Philippines Embassy
50N Nyaya Marg,
Chanakyapuri
Tel: 608-492/608-842

Portuguese Embassy
A-24 Westend Colony
Tel: 674-596

Saudi Arabian Embassy
S-347 Panchsheel Park
Tel: 644-5054

Singapore High Commission
E-6 Chandragupta Marg,
Chanakyapuri
Tel: 608-149/604-162

Spanish Embassy
12 Prithvi Raj Road
Tel: 301-5892/301-3834

Sri Lanka High Commission
27 Kautilya Marg,
Chanakyapuri
Tel: 301-0201/301-0202

Swedish Embassy
Nyaya Marg,
Chanakyapuri
Tel: 604-961/604-011

Swiss Embassy
Nyaya Marg,
Chanakyapuri
Tel: 604-225/604-226

Thailand Embassy
56-N Nyaya Marg,
Chanakyapuri
Tel: 607-807/607-289

U.S.S.R Embassy
Shanti Path,
Chanakyapuri
Tel: 605-875/606-026

U.S.A Embassy
Shanti Path,
Chanakyapuri
Tel: 600-651

Vietnamese Embassy
2 Navjeevan Vihar
Tel: 669-843

FURTHER READING

History and Religion

Balsham, A.L: *The Wonder That Was India,* London, 1967, reprint 1985.

Gandhi, M.K.: *An Autobiography or The Story of My Experiments With Truth*, first published 1927-9, London 1982.

Gascoigne, B.: *The Great Mughals*, London 1979.

Hibbert, C.: *The History of the Indian Mutiny*, London, 1978.

Keays, John: *Into India*, 1973.

Moorehouse, G: *India Britannica*, London, 1983 and Calcutta, London

Spear, P. and Thapar, R.: *A History of India, vols 1 and 2*, 1978.

Watson, F.: *A Concise History of India*, London 1974.

Novels, Travel Writing and Commentaries

Allen, Charles, ed: *Plain Tales From The Raj*, London, 1973.

Cameron, James: *Indian Summer*, London, 1974.

Collins, L and Lapierre, D: *Freedom At Midnight*, India, 1976.

Farrell, E.M.: *The Siege of Krishnapur.*

Fishlock, Trevor: *India File*, London 1983

Forster, E.M.: *Passage To India*, London, 1924.

Naipaul, V.S.: *An Area Of Darkness*, London, 1964 and India 1990. *A Wounded Civilization*, London, 1977.

Theroux, Paul: *Great Railway Bazaar*, London, 1980.

A

Abdu'n Nabi's Mosque, 74
Adham Khan, 58
ahimsa, 73
akara (wrestling pit), 72
Alai Darwaza, 36
amla, 51
Archaelogical Survey, 65
Ashokan pillar, 58, 73
attar (rose-oil essense), 72, 99
ayahs (nannies), 69
ayanas, 46

B

Baba Kharak Singh Marg, 94
Babur, 14, 17
Baha'i Temple, 74
baingan mumtaz, 86
Baker, Herbert, 16, 22, 24
baoli, 59
Bara Gumbad, 69
Baroda House, 56
bhandej, 94
Bharatpur's Keoladeo National Park, 83
bidri, 47
Bird Hospital, 31
biryani, 82, 86
British magazine, 60
Buland Darwaza, 83`
burfi halwan, 87
burqua, 31, 71

C

Chadni Chowk, 15, 31, 49, 52, 94, 103
cassata, 67
catechu, 87
chatris, 64
Chatta Chowk, 28
chhatris, 23
chikan, 48
Church Mission Rd, 49, 50
coolies, 50
Coronation Memorial, 63
coupe, 17
Crafts mela, 77
Crafts Museum, 43
crewel, 94

D

dal makhanai, 26, 86
damaru (drum, sometimes made from human skulls), 48
dargah (shrine), 45
Dariba Kalam, 32
Delhi Zoo, 43
dhaba, 48
dhabas, 75
dhal, 68
dharma, 73
dhurries, 96
Digambar Jani Temple, 31
Discos, 78
Diwan-i-Am (hall of public audience), 28
Diwan-i-Khas (hall of private audience), 30
dosas, 85, 89

F

Fatehpur Masjid, 49
Fatehpur Sikri, 82
Fazullah, Shaikh (famous poet), 58
feezes, 71
feringhi (foreigners), 60
Feroz Shah Kotta, 73
firdaus gorma (lamb curry), 70, 89
Flagstaff Tower, 62

G

Gadodia Market, 50
gajar ka halwa, 87
gali batasha (sugar meringue street), 51
Gandhi Memorial Museum, 76
Gandhi, Muhatma, 19, 47, 75, 94
garam masala, 70
Ghantewala (Bell ringer), 52
ghazals (songs), 88
ghee (clarified butter), 32, 53, 89
Gujari (Gujarat), 46
gulab jamun (spongy ground-almond balls), 52, 87
Guru Granth Sahib (Sikh Bible), 53
Gushtaba, 86

123

H

hammans (bath), 31
Hanuman Mandir, 46
havelis (merchant's house) 15, 50, 66
Himachal Pradesh, 46
Hindu Ras's House, 62
hookah, 37,45, 60, 98
Humayan's Tomb, 44
Hyderabad House, 56

I, J

idlies, 45, 85, 86, 89
ikat, 46, 94
India Gate, 22
Indra Gandhi (first woman Prime Minister), 19, 38
Indra Gandhi Memorial, 38
International Dolls Museum, 74
jaggery (yellow mud), 51
jalebi, 45, 87
jali, 83
Jama Masjid, 26,33, 70, 83
Jami Masjid, 73
Janpath, 25, 93, 97
Jantar Mantar, 24
Jawaharlal Nehru (first Prime Minister), 19

K

kacha (boxer shorts), 53
Kadai Paneer, 34
kahtte aloo, 86
kaju-ki-barfi, 52
kakoni kebab, 88
kangha, 53
kanglin (flutes made from human shin bones), 48
kankan (steel bangle), 53
karah, 52
Kashmiri Gate, 61
Kasturba Gandhi Marg, 56
katoris, 45
kebabs, 38, 88
kesh (hair locks), 53
Khadi Gramodyog Bhawan, 47
khadi, 16, 46, 94
Khairu'l-Manazi Masjid, 43
Khameeri roli, 70, 84
Khari Baoli, 49
Khas Mahal, 30
Khirki Masjid, 67
khumba (potter's workshop), 97
Khuni Darwaza (woody gate), 74
Khwabagh (house of dreams), 83
Kinari Bazaar (braid-shop street), 32
kirpan (ceremonial dagger), 53
kolam, 43
kotwali, 52
kulcha, 34, 86
kuleha, 70
kulfi, 87
Kushk-i-Feroz, 73

M

madrasa (college for Islamic studies), 37
Mahabharat, 12, 17, 41
maqsura (screen), 36
masala dosas, 45
masala, 47
matkas (water pots), 97
memsahibs, 62
Metcalfe House, 63
Metcalfe's Folly, 58
Metcalfe, Sir Thomas, 37, 58, 63
misri chini (crystal), 51
mojadis (slippers), 99
Moti Masjid (Pearl Mosque), 29
Mountbatten, Lord Louis, 24
Mughal Gardens, 24
Mumtaz Mahal, 29
musumbi (sweet lime), 22, 45
Mutiny Memorial, 62

N, O

naam, 70,80, 86
Nagaland, 46
nahari (morning lamb curry), 70, 84
Naher-i-Bahist (street of paradise), 29
Nai Sarak (New Street), 33, 66
Nakkar Khana (royal drum-house), 28
namadas, 48, 96
National Gallery of Modern Art, 56
National Museum, 54
nautch (courtesan dancers), 66
nav-ratan (mine gems), 86
neem (sticks used as toothbrushes), 51
Netaji Subhash Park, 72
Nicholson Cemetery, 61
Nicholson, Bungadier-General John, 61
Ochterlony, Sir David, 60

P

paam wallahs, 87
paan, 31, 50, 87
Panch Mahal, 83
papadoms (puffed wheat), 68
Paratha Wallah Gully (alley of breadseller), 53
paratha, 54
paschesi (game similar to ludo), 83
pasha, 60
pasta, 91
patta, 47
phool-makhana (Indian popcorn), 51
pieta dura, 81, 83, 97
Poompahar (Tamil Nadu), 46
potola, 94
prasad (white coated marbles), 51
puja (worship), 46, 52
pukka, 62
pulao, 71
Purana Qila, 40
purdah, 45, 83
puri, 68, 87

Q

Qal'a-i-Khuna Masjid, 41, 42
qawwalis (mystic's songs), 45
Qudsia Bagh, 61
Qutb-minar, 34, 36
Qutb-und-din-Aibak, 13, 17, 35
Quwwat-ul-Islam Masjid, 36

R

raan, 88
Rail Musuem, 68
Raisana Hill, 22
Raj Ghat, 76
Rajpath, 22
rakhi (decorative tinned threads), 102
Ramayana, 103
Rang Mahal, 30
rasgulla (cream cheese balls coated in sugared rose water), 82, 87
Red Fort, 27
reeshmi kebab (minced chicken), 26
reetha, 51
rogan josh (curried lamb), 82
roomali roti, 38, 70, 86

S

saag paneer (dish of spiced cottage cheese and spinach), 75
saag, 87
Safdarjang's Tomb, 38
Saint James Church, 60
sambhar, 87
samovars, 48, 98
sani, 55, 94
Sansad Bhawan, 24
Sansad Marg (Parliament Street), 24
Seekh Kebab Malai, 34
seekh kebabs, 70, 86, 89
Shah Jahan, 14, 27, 29, 30, 32, 33
shahi paneer, 86
Shahjahanabad, 26

shahtush (shawls), 48
shammi, 70, 89
Shanti Vana (Forest of Peace), 76
Sharadhanand Marg, 51
sheermal, 70
Sher Mandal, 41
sitar, 38, 88
Skinner, Col. James, 60
South Minaret, 34
Stein, Sir Marc Aurel, 55
subze (spiced vegetable), 54
Sundar Nagar Government Nursery, 44
Sunder Nagar Market, 95
Suraj Kund, 77
Surya, 77

T

Taj Mahal, 14, 15, 18, 27, 30, 44, 75, 80, 82
tandoori kebabs, 82
tandoori, 25, 93, 97
tankas (religious paintings in silk), 48
tatties, 25
Teen Murti House (residence of India's first Prime Minister), 76
Telegraph Memorial, 60
thali, 68, 82, 85, 89
Tibet House, 69
tikka, 88
toga, 55
Tughlaqabad Fort, 57

U, V, Y, Z

Ugrasen-ki-Baoli (step well), 56
uttapams, 45
vark (leaves of edible silver), 51
Vijay Ghat Memorial, 77
vindaloo, 89
yakatori, 90
zabaglione, 91
zenana (harem quarters), 83

ART / PHOTO CREDITS

Photography

10, 52	**Image Vault**
80	**Toby Sinclair**
82	**Roberto Meazza**
85	**APA Photo Agency**
103	**J.L. Nou**
100 above	**Avinash Pasricha**
100 below	**Luca Invernezzi**
101 below	**R.K. Goyal**
Maps	**Berndtson & Berndtson**
Cover Design	**Klaus Geisler**

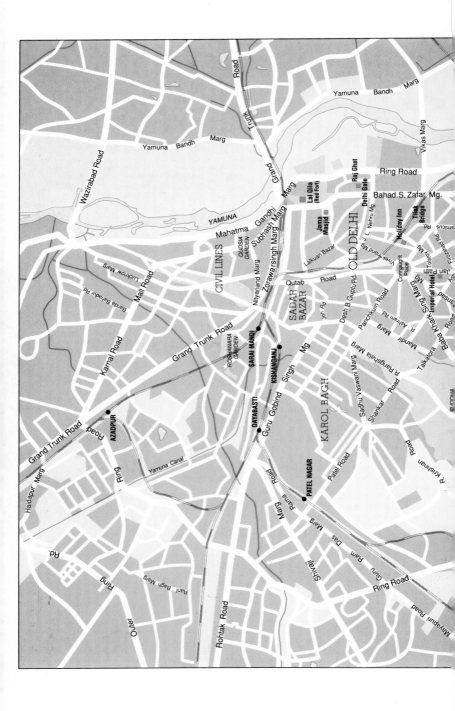